DATE DUE

AP 22 '00			
MR 5 '01			
MR 01 '04			

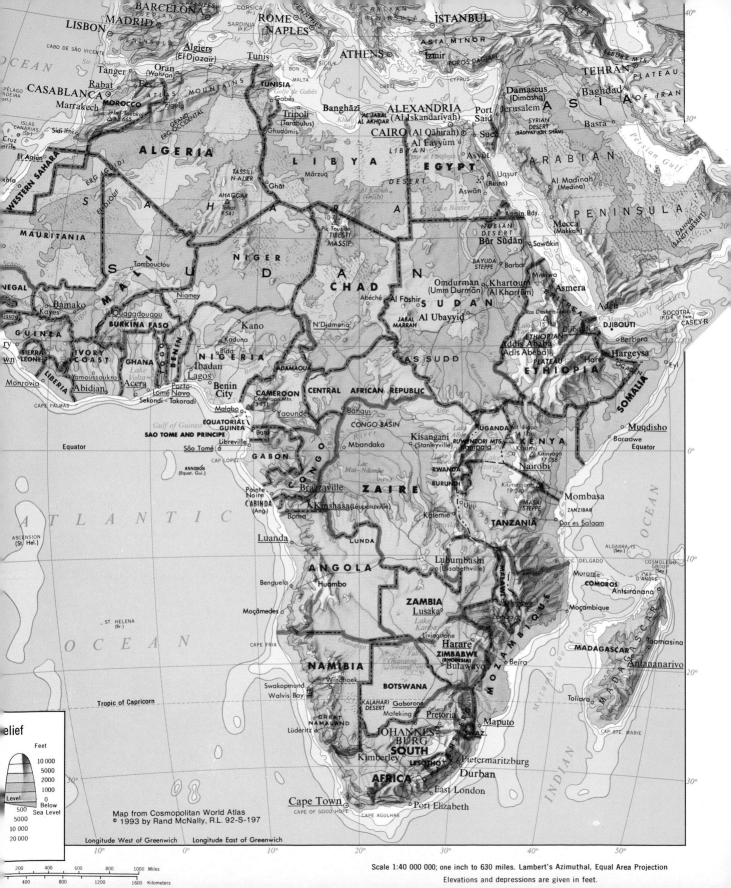

ATLANTIC

OCEAN

N'zeto • Nova Caipemba • Sanza Pombo • Kahemba • Luiza • Chitato • Kaniama • Kabongo • Muyumba

Ambriz • Uíge • Negage • Camissombo • Kapanga • Kamina

Luanda • Caxito • Camabatela • Marimba • Luremo • Caúngula • Chiluage • Bukama • Luena

PONTA DAS PALMEIRINHAS • Catete • N'dalatando • Malanje • Saurimo • Muconda • Malonge • Kasaji • Dilolo • Tenke • Lubudi

Barra do Cuanza • Muxima • Dondo • Cambundi-Catembo • Cacólo • KATANGA

Porto Amboim • Sabela • ANGOLA • Waku Kundo • Camacupa • Luena • Munhango • Cazombo • Calunda • Mwinilunga • Solwezi • Kipu

Sumbe • Bailundo • Kuito • Cangombe • Balovale • Kasempa

Lobito • Serra Môco 2620 • Caála • Huambo (Nova Lisboa) • Ganda • Chitembo • Lumbala N'guimbo • Mussuma • Lukulu

Benguela • Caconda • Kaoma • Mumbw

CABO DE SANTA MARIA • Kuvango • Menongue • Cando • Kalabo • Mongu

Lucira • Bibala • Lubango • Capelongo • Cassinga • Cuito-Cuanavale • Mavinga • Senanga

Namibe • Cassinga • Caiundo • Neriquinha • Choma • Kalomo

Tombua • Humbe • Xangongo • Ondjiva • Cuangar • Dirico • Sesheke • Kazungula • Livingstone

PONTA DA MARCA • Chitado • Cuangar • CAPRIVI ZIPFEL • Hwar

Foz do Cunene • Rehoboth • Ondangwa • Shakawe • MABABE DEPRESSION

CAPE FRIA • OVAMBOLAND • Etosha Pan • KAUKAU VELD • OKAVANGO DELTA

KAOKO VELD • Sesfontein • Namutoni • Maun

Okaukuejo • Tsumeb • Tsau • Totong • Makgadikgadi

Otavi • Grootfontein • Lake Ngami

Outjo • Lake Xau • Francis

Otjiwarongo • Ghanzi

2574 Brandberg • NAMIBIA • BOTSWANA

Omaruru • Tshwaane • Serowe

Karibib • Okahandja • Epokiro • Shoshong

Usakos • Gobabis • KALAHARI

Swakopmund • DAMARALAND • Windhoek • Lehututu • Tshane • Molepolole • Mochu

Walvisbaai Walvis Bay • Rehoboth • DESERT • Gaborone

Tropic of Capricorn • Tsumis Park • Khakhea • Kanye • BOPHU

HOLLANDSBIRD ISLAND • Maltahöhe • Mariental • BOPHUTHATSWAN

Gibeon • Zeerust • Rustenburg

GREAT NAMAQUALAND • Koes • Tshabong • Mmabatho • Mafikeng • Krugers

Lüderitz • Bethanien • Keetmanshoop • JOHANNES

Aus • Guibes • Seeheim • Aroab • Askham • Vryburg • Potchefstroom • Klerksdorp

Karasburg • Kakamas • Hotazel • Kuruman • Bloemhof • Odendaalsrus • Virginia

Oranjemund • Warmbad • Upington • Makwassie • Warrenton

Alexander Bay • Pofadder • Kenhardt • Sishen • Kimberley

Port Nolloth • BUSHMAN LAND • Kakamas • Prieska • Hopetown • Jagersfontein • Bloemfontein

Okiep • Springbok • Kenhardt • Springfontein

Garies • Grootvloer • Verneukpan • SOUTH • De Aar • Colesberg • Burgersdorp • Barkly Ea

Kamieskroon • Brandvlei • Britstown • Noupoort • Aliwal

Bitterfontein • Carnarvon • AFRICA • Middelburg • Sterkstroom • Tarkastad • Que

Kompasberg 2504 • Victoria West • Murraysburg

Map from New International Atlas
© 1993 by Rand McNally, R.L. 92-S-197

Enchantment of the World

NAMIBIA

By Jason Lauré

Consultant for Namibia: Tji-Tjai J. Uanivi, Ph.D. Candidate, Department of History, Rutgers University, New Brunswick, New Jersey

Consultant for Reading: Robert L. Hillerich, Ph.D., Visiting Professor, University of South Florida; Consultant, Pinellas County Schools, Florida

CHILDRENS PRESS ®
CHICAGO

Meerkats, or suricates, live in Etosha National Park.

Project Editor: Mary Reidy
Design: Margrit Fiddle

Library of Congress Cataloging-in-Publication Data

Lauré, Jason.
    Namibia / by Jason Lauré.
        p.   cm. — (Enchantment of the world)
    Includes index.
    Summary: Describes the geography, history, people, and
culture of Namibia.
    ISBN 0-516-02615-1
    1. Namibia—Juvenile literature. 2. Namibia.
I. Title. II. Series.
DT1519.L38 1993   92-39137
968.81—dc20   CIP
                                        AC

SECOND PRINTING, 1994.
Copyright © 199 ⸝ by Childrens Press®, Inc.
All rights reserved. Published simultaneously in Canada.
Printed in the United States of America.
    2 3 4 5 6 7 8 9 10 R 02 01 00 99 98 97 96 95 94

Picture Acknowledgments
The Bettmann Archive: 20 (bottom), 28
Historical Pictures/Stock Montage: 20 (top), 22
Impact Visuals: © **Eliason/Link,** 5; © **Afrapik/Guy Tillim,**
53; © **Link,** 64 (2 photos); © **Tom Benton,** 108
Lauré Communications: © **David Coulson,** 6, 8 (2 photos),
9, 10 (left), 12 (2 photos), 13, 27, 56 (2 photos), 70
(bottom), 73 (left), 74 (2 photos), 75 (right), 78, 79 (left), 80
(2 photos), 91, 92 (left), 93 (right), 97, 101; © **Jason Lauré**
Cover Inset, 10 (right), 19, 36, 40, 42, 45 (2 photos), 47
(2 photos), 50 (2 photos), 57, 60, 62, 63, (2 photos), 68
(right), 83 (2 photos), 84 (2 photos), 85, 86 (top), 88
(4 photos), 89 (2 photos), 90 (3 photos), 99 (3 photos), 100,
102 (right), 103 (2 photos), 104 (2 photos), 112 (right);
© **Ettagale Blauer,** 68 (left)
North Wind Picture Archives: 31
Photri: Cover, 14, 30, 75 (center); © **Gerald Cubitt,** 66
(2 photos), 69, 70 (top), 75 (left), 81, 93 (left), 95
(2 photos), 102 (left); © **ABY,** 72 (top left), 86 (bottom)
Reuters/Bettmann: 51, 52, 54 (2 photos), 96, 112 (left), 114
Tony Stone Worldwide/Chicago: © **Brian Seed,** 16
SuperStock International, Inc.: © **Martin Bruce,** 4, 72 (top
right, bottom left and right), 73 (right), 92 (right)
UPI/Bettmann: 26, 32, 34, 43, 48
Valan: © **Fred Bruemmer,** 76, 77 (right), 79 (right);
© **Stephen J. Krasemann,** 77 (left)
Len W. Meents: Maps on 57, 73, 76, 93
**Courtesy Flag Research Center, Winchester,
Massachusetts 01890:** Flag on back cover
Cover: Sand dunes and bush, Namib-Naukluft National
Park
Cover Inset: View of Windhoek

Amethysts are mined in the north around Tsumeb.

TABLE OF CONTENTS

Chapter 1

THE NATURAL ENVIRONMENT

GEOGRAPHY

Namibia, which became an independent nation on March 21, 1990, is a sparsely populated country covering 317,818 square miles (823,145 square kilometers). It lies in the southwest portion of Africa, its western border marked by a 950-mile (1,529-kilometer) coastline on the Atlantic Ocean. To the north it is bounded by Angola and Zambia, to the east by Botswana, and to the south by South Africa. It is a land of desert and dunes, disappearing streams and lakes, and a small, but rapidly growing, population of nearly 1.8 million.

The country is roughly rectangular in shape, with the exception of the Caprivi Strip, a narrow piece of land along the country's northern border that extends Namibia's territory for 250 miles (402 kilometers) to the east. The strip varies from 25 to 65 miles (40 to 105 kilometers) wide. This length of land extends Namibia's northern border to the center of southern Africa, touching on Zambia to the northeast and Botswana to the east, and reaching almost to Victoria Falls.

The geography and climate of Namibia make it a harsh and demanding place in which to live. Much of the land is desert. The

Opposite page: Oshanas, *dry watercourses that flow after rains, sustain small plants in the desert.*

The Namib (left) is a strip of desert along the Atlantic coast. Brandberg (right) is the highest point in Namibia.

coastal shelf, a strip of desert called the Namib, extends along the entire Atlantic coastline, stretching 56 to 93 miles (90 to 150 kilometers) inland. There it abruptly meets the plateau that dominates the central interior of the country. The plateau averages 4,000 feet (1,219 meters) in altitude. The capital city, Windhoek, is situated at 5,428 feet (1,654 meters), slightly lower than the highest point in the country, Brandberg (8,465 feet; 2,580 meters). The central plateau, which dominates the middle of the country, gradually slopes away to the east and north. Much of the remaining eastern portion of the country gives way to the sandy stretches of the Kalahari Desert. It is also called simply *Omaheke*, which means ''desert'' in the Herero language. The Kalahari is almost barren of life, marked only by scrubby bushes and grasses.

CLIMATE

While the central plateau has a pleasant climate, the Atlantic coastline of Namibia is a climate of extremes. While the land in

Morning fog rolls over the sand dunes.

this area is a true desert, with sand dunes and virtually no rainfall, the cold Benguela Current sweeping in off the ocean keeps the coast cool and damp. In place of rain, a morning fog rolls in off the ocean most days of the year. As the fog rolls over the dunes of the Namib Desert, it quickly evaporates, and the land becomes searingly hot.

A person standing at the exact point where the fog evaporates feels cold when facing the ocean and hot when facing inland. Where rain does fall, mostly in the northern part of the central plateau, it falls in great torrents and then quickly dries up. Temperatures can reach as high as 104 degrees Fahrenheit (40 degrees Celsius), then plunge downward as soon as the sun goes down. Nights can be bitterly cold.

RIVERS

The northern and southern borders of Namibia are marked by rivers. The Okavango River, which forms part of Namibia's

The Kunene River (above), is part of Namibia's northern border and the Orange River (inset) forms the southern border.

northern border, flows across the Caprivi Strip. The Kunene flows for about 200 miles (322 kilometers) along the northern border and empties into the Atlantic Ocean. The Orange River forms Namibia's southern border.

The water that does exist in much of Namibia is rarely visible. There are no permanent rivers within the country. Instead, there are numerous dry watercourses, called *oshanas* in the Ovambo and Herero languages. These are depressions in the earth where rivers flow briefly after the rains. Even after a very heavy rain, the rivers rarely flow for more than two or three days, but within the earth the moisture remains for much longer periods. This moisture sustains the life of the small plants that manage to survive in the desert.

There are a few lakes in the country. Two notable ones are Lakes Otjikoto and Guinas, both of them in the north near the mining town of Tsumeb. Water, or lack of it, has always limited the development of the country. Drought is more the natural condition than the exception.

THE NAMIB

The Namib Desert occupies 15 percent of the land. *Namib* means "endless expanse" in the language of the San. Although the Namib is a true desert, its position next to the Atlantic Ocean where the cold Benguela Current flows gives it a unique weather pattern. The moisture that rolls over the land in the form of fog allows small creatures to survive in this harsh land. They wait at the top of the sand dunes, catching each drop of water that condenses from the fog. The ridge of the dunes is the point at which cold ocean air meets hot desert air.

The dunes have been on the move for thousands of years. The constant wind, coming off the ocean, pushes at the dunes and blows grains of sand up and over the top. These grains ripple down the other side of the dunes, joining with hundreds of thousands of others, all of them polished to a smooth round shape. The dunes here appear purple in the sunlight because the sand has been coated with a red iron oxide from the ocean fog. The dunes can reach a height of 984 feet (300 meters), but as they are always moving, their size is likewise always changing.

The vegetation and the desert creatures are easily overlooked against the vast, brown landscape of the Namib. For hundreds of miles, to the horizon and beyond, there appears to be nothing alive here. It doesn't seem possible that anyone or anything could live in such a bare environment. Yet, in some areas of the coast, where the wind blows from different directions, the dunes have very steep sides with nearly flat tops and move much more

Constant winds change the shapes of the dunes in the Namib Desert.
A chameleon (inset) is almost the same color as the sand.

slowly. This gives desert vegetation a place to grow. Small desert
creatures, mainly insects, rodents, and snakes, survive here
through extraordinary adaptations to the climate. They burrow
beneath the top layers of the sand, taking advantage of the cool
temperatures they find there.

Even more surprising, the region manages to sustain much
larger animal life. Scattered through the regions, in small
numbers, live a variety of jackals, hyenas, ostriches, and even
elephants and giraffes. These animals get their food and water
from the plants that use the wet coastal fog to keep alive. The
plants send roots down into the sandy soil where they find
moisture that is trapped below the surface. Many animals gain all
the moisture they need from the leaves of the plants they eat.

A wrecked ship along Skeleton Coast

Only those plants and creatures, including people, that have adapted to live in such conditions are able to survive in these regions.

SKELETON COAST

Along with the harsh climate, Namibia also has a dangerous coastline. It is so difficult to navigate that it has earned the name "Skeleton Coast," because so many ships have been dashed against the rocks and destroyed. These ships may be seen along the coast, usually lying on their sides. What makes this area even more treacherous today are the ships that were torn apart by violent storms and then sank. Those that are relatively close to shore add to the hazards of sailing along the coastline. The stretch of coastline that is known as the Skeleton Coast runs from the Kunene River southward to Cape Cross.

Rock drawings at Twyfelfontein

Chapter 2

EARLY HISTORY

EARLIEST POPULATIONS

The history of settlements in the area now called Namibia, but known throughout much of its history as South West Africa, begins with the San and the Khoikhoi peoples. Unlike other African territories, part of South West Africa has been continually inhabited by the same people from the earliest known times. The San left a clear record of their history through rock drawings that have been perfectly preserved by the extremely dry climate.

The Damara group were already living in the north central part of the area when the cattle-owning Herero people began migrating from the area around present-day Botswana (east of Namibia) in the early sixteenth century. The original home of the Herero is believed to have been around the Rift Valley in East Africa. The Nama had come up from the south at about the same time. Through the years, up to about 1830, these peoples were frequently on the move as more powerful people displaced weaker groups. Migration into the region was from all directions: north, south, and east. (The ocean forms the western border and no visitors arrived that way until the time of the Europeans.) Migrants usually came looking for better grazing for their animals or to escape domination by Europeans arriving in South Africa.

The San use bows and arrows for hunting.

Fighting between these groups was sometimes quite fierce and often forced retreats into less desirable territory. By the time the Europeans started to look with interest at South West Africa, many Africans had already settled in the area around Windhoek.

EUROPEANS REACH PRESENT-DAY NAMIBIA

Portuguese explorers, sailing down the west coast of Africa, were the first whites to reach present-day Namibia. Portuguese explorations along the coast of Africa are well documented. The Portuguese were able to navigate the treacherous waters along the coastline and in 1484 marked their arrival by placing a stone cross just north of what is today the town of Swakopmund. Two years later, in 1486, Bartholomew Dias landed on a spot he called *Angra Pequena*, which means "narrow bay." Today it is the town of Luderitz.

The Portuguese did not make any attempt to establish themselves in the territory as they did in other west African areas where they settled and ultimately established colonies. The severe climate, which kept the population very small, made this area unappealing to the Portuguese. They preferred to claim areas that offered a supply of laborers and people they could enslave.

Other whites, mainly British and Afrikaners (whites of Dutch descent) from South Africa, heard about large cattle herds kept by the Herero and Nama people in South West Africa and began making trips into the territory to try to establish trade with them. (South Africa had already been colonized by Europeans.) Others went into the interior to find copper deposits they had heard about. All of these visitors stayed for brief periods and then left, often relating wild stories about the people who lived in the area. Permanent settlement was left mainly to the missionaries, who began arriving in earnest in the early nineteenth century.

MISSIONARIES MOVE IN

The Wesleyans (Methodists) had opened a mission among the Nama people in Warmbad, just north of the Orange River, in 1834, but soon gave it up. In 1842, the Rhenish Missionary Society took over this station, and with the encouragement of the Afrikaners who had established themselves in the central region of South West Africa, they created a mission in Herero territory. The Rhenish Mission expanded over the next decades, becoming the first important German presence in the territory. This eventually encouraged Germany to claim the area. The mission stations were scattered all over the vast territory, from Warmbad in the south, up through the central plateau, and as far as Otavi in the north.

The missionaries were not very successful at converting the people or changing their way of life, so they turned instead to establish a mission trading company. This led them to become involved with many of the political and military problems of the people. They came to play a direct role in conflicts between the peoples. The missions were more successful as trading companies, in part because they had established themselves over such a wide expanse of the territory.

INTERNAL ETHNIC WARS

Internal ethnic wars were a fact of life during these years as each group tried to gain territory for itself. Although there were huge tracts of unoccupied land, few areas were suitable for intensive grazing for cattle. Newcomers to any area came into conflict with the people already there. The Ovambo lived far to the north, with the Herero to the south of them. The cattle-raising Herero were often on the move seeking out grazing lands. They moved slowly southward. In time, they found their way into the land of the Damara, a people with no strong central organization who were easily conquered.

At the same time, groups of Nama people were moving northward. They had left Cape Colony in South Africa when the Europeans began expanding their communities. The Nama were also cattle-raising people and they soon came into conflict with the Herero. The Nama defeated the Herero in 1840 and pushed them back, north of the Swakop River.

In 1863, the Herero and Nama began fighting again. The Herero were stronger, but in the end there was no clear winner. Both sides used up a great deal of their resources in warfare. They were left vulnerable to a more powerful enemy—the Europeans.

The Germans were not the only European power that desired

The German architectural influence can be seen in this pre-World War II photograph of Windhoek.

South West Africa. The Afrikaner farmers of South Africa had begun moving into the lands of the Herero. In the 1870s the Herero chief, Maharero, turned to the British governor of the Cape Colony in South Africa, Sir Henry Barkly, for protection.

Trade routes were already established in the territory. Cattle were one of the main exports. They were shipped out of Walvis Bay, the territory's only deep-water port. The Europeans also expected to earn money from the mining concessions they established in the territory, but during this period, around the middle 1800s, this was little more than a hope. Indeed, in 1858, the Nama chiefs were united in their desire not to sell any of their land to whites coming up from Cape Colony. They agreed that no one should allow mining in their territory. But in the 1880s and 1890s the chiefs began to sell their land and cattle.

In 1884 German Chancellor
Otto von Bismarck (right)
assembled Europeans at the
Berlin West African Conference
(above) to protect Germany's claim
over African lands.

Chapter 3

THE COLONIAL ERA

GERMANS CLAIM SOUTH WEST AFRICA

In 1878, the British occupied Walvis Bay, and claimed it for Cape Colony. This left South West Africa with no control over its only deep-water port. The Germans, who had explored very little of the territory, responded by placing all of South West Africa under their protection.

In 1883, a German merchant, Adolf Luderitz, bought the land around Angra Pequena to ensure the use of that harbor. It was a very poor second to Walvis Bay.

To protect their claim over South West Africa and other African territories, in 1884 the German Chancellor Otto von Bismarck called the European powers to the "Berlin West African Conference." This conference met periodically from November 1884 through February 1885. The European powers sorted out their various claims to parts of Africa. They agreed to draw their version of the map of Africa so as to avoid conflicts among themselves. Some of their claims were based on treaties they had secured with African chiefs. But much of what the Europeans claimed was backed up by nothing except the desire to expand their empires in Africa.

German troops embarking for Namibia in 1881

When the Germans, Portuguese, British, French, and Belgians claimed territory, they did so with the arrogant assumption that they had a right to do so. At no time did they consult with any of the Africans who lived in the lands they were claiming. The Germans laid claim to South West Africa, which was defined as the land between the Orange River and the Kunene. The Kunene formed the border with the Portuguese colony of Angola. Germany also claimed Tanganyika, in East Africa, and had a brief fantasy about someday joining these two territories.

During the brief time in which Germany ruled South West Africa, it created many problems for the Africans. The Ovambo and Herero people, who lived on both sides of the Kunene River, now found themselves divided between German South West Africa and Portuguese Angola.

STRUGGLE FOR CONTROL

The record of German rule over South West Africa is one of brutal force and a total disregard for the native people. German soldiers were brought into the territory in 1889 to prepare for the fight for control of South West Africa. The new German chancellor, Count von Caprivi, made plain his intention to control South West Africa no matter what the cost in lives or money. Though most of the lives that were lost were African, it was not for lack of leadership among the local people. The cost to the Germans in human life was high, too. In 1890, von Caprivi declared he would control South West Africa "at all costs."

AFRICAN LEADERS RESIST

Both the Nama and the Herero had intelligent and strong leaders in their fight against the Germans. Chief Hendrik Samuel Witbooi, the Nama leader who possessed great military skill, led his troops, armed with modern rifles, against the Germans. In the early 1890s, he was able to unite various Nama groups and fought against the Germans for years, at one time forcing the Germans to sign a peace treaty. The success was short-lived, however, and the Germans virtually wiped out the Nama in later fighting. Samuel Maharero, the Herero's strong leader, likewise fought against the Germans, forcing them to bring in more and more men from Europe.

The governor of the territory, Theodor Leutwein, appointed by the German chancellor in 1898, had no understanding of the people he was ruling. Leutwein truly believed that the Africans welcomed the arrival of the Germans and would give up their freedom and their way of life without a fight. Leutwein assumed that the Germans had a right to the land and that the Africans would accept this drastic change in their lives.

Leutwein conducted a long correspondence with Witbooi. The

intent on each side was quite different. Leutwein was the representative of a government that intended to colonize South West Africa, while Witbooi believed that he and his people should be treated exactly as the Europeans treated other European powers. Witbooi never accepted the German attempt to control the land of his people. The stage was set for the devastating and bitter war that would follow.

FIGHTING FOR CATTLE AND LAND

Of all the many differences between the Germans and the Africans, particularly the Herero, it was the different attitudes toward cattle and land that finally led to war. The Herero counted their wealth in cattle, like many Africans, and expanded their herds as much as the dry climate permitted. These larger herds required more and more grazing land, and in South West Africa, grazing land was scarce.

At the same time, the Germans were trying to build up their cattle business. They saw cattle as temporary possessions to be turned into wealth through the sale of their meat and hides.

ASSESSING THE ENEMY

The solution to the problem was quite clear to the Germans. They would do away with the Herero and their cattle. This would leave the more docile peoples, who would provide the Germans with the labor they needed for their large farms. The plan was clearly spelled out in a written document by Dr. Richard Hindorf. He had come to South West Africa to advise the German businessmen how to get the most out of their investment in the territory. Hindorf concluded that the only way to make South West Africa pay its own way was to get rid of the people and practices that did not fit the German government's plan.

The basic plan—reducing the size of the native herds of cattle—began in earnest. In the Nama territories, grazing land was sold to Europeans and the Nama gradually became hired laborers. Natural catastrophes also helped reduce the size of the herds. Droughts and famines prevailed, and an outbreak of rinderpest, a disease that strikes cattle, proved devastating. The loss of cattle forced the Nama to sell their land to buy food.

HERERO-GERMAN WAR

The situation with the Herero, however, was quite a different matter. During the next few years, the Germans systematically set about taking over Herero grazing lands and their cattle. By 1903, they had secured more than half of the Herero's cattle and had taken so much land that finally the Herero had to fight for survival.

The Herero War against the Germans broke out on January 12, 1904 at Okahandja under the leadership of Samuel Maharero. He and his troops attacked the Germans.

The Herero were well organized, intelligent, and well led. They inflicted a great deal of damage on the Germans. The Herero were able to disrupt both the railroad between Windhoek and Swakopmund and telegraph communications. The German General von Trotha ordered that the Herero nation be exterminated.

Inside German territory (which South West Africa was considered) every Herero, armed or unarmed, with or without

Kaiser Wilhelm II

cattle, was to be shot. No women or children were allowed in the territory. They were to be driven back or fired on.

HERERO DEFEATED

The Germans nearly succeeded in carrying out the order, although not without a price. In all, the Germans lost five thousand soldiers and settlers and spent a great amount of money trying to hold on to the territory. Eventually, the Herero were reduced to a few hundred men fighting against fourteen thousand German troops. Although thousands of Herero were defeated by the German soldiers, by the end of 1905 it was estimated that fifteen thousand Herero survived out of an original population of about seventy thousand. About 75 to 80 percent of the Herero had died. Small numbers continued to fight in the south until 1907.

The Nama, who joined in the revolt in October 1904, also suffered great losses. They lost an estimated 35 to 50 percent of

The discovery of diamonds in 1908

their people, including Hendrik Witbooi, who was killed in battle in October 1905. In addition to the human loss, the Africans were left almost entirely without cattle, a means to start life again. As a result of both these losses, the Africans were left without their traditions, their customs, and their standards of living. Their way of life in South West Africa had ended.

By the end of 1905, Kaiser Wilhelm II of Germany signed an order that expropriated all land and cattle. The people who remained were starving. The Germans had been so thorough in their attack, they found themselves without a work force when the war was over.

By 1907, the Germans were ready to profit from their bloody investment in South West Africa. In 1908 diamonds were discovered, the first substantial indication of the territory's mineral wealth. The small European community, numbering only fourteen thousand, had only a few years of peace. In 1914 World War I began in Europe. The echoes of this war were soon heard in Africa.

*An 1899 drawing shows
the British charging
against the Afrikaners.*

Chapter 4

AFTER GERMAN RULE

GERMANS DEFEATED

Although the war in Europe was thousands of miles away, the European colonists in Africa were drawn into it. They took sides and fought out their parts of the war on African soil. The biggest British presence in the region was in the British Crown Colony of South Africa. It had been united only a dozen years earlier.

South Africa was composed of two groups of European colonists who fiercely opposed each other — the English-speaking people and the people known as Boers, or Afrikaners. There was such hostility that a war broke out in 1899. It took British troops, which finally numbered nearly a half million soldiers, to defeat the Afrikaners. The war ended with the Treaty of Vereeniging in 1902.

After this brutal war, the Germans in South West Africa thought the Afrikaners would not fight against them, alongside the British. The Germans even thought the Afrikaners would fight on their side. But the British and Afrikaners had managed to heal the wounds of their own war. By the time World War I began, the South African colonists were united against the Germans.

There were only two thousand regular German soldiers and about seven thousand armed German colonists in South West Africa at this time. The South Africans organized forty thousand men, both British and Afrikaners, who overwhelmed Windhoek. After a battle that began in April and ended in July 1915, the Germans in South West Africa were completely defeated. South West Africa was now firmly in the hands of the South African colonists. The defeated Germans were allowed to return to their homes and farms.

The South Africans wanted to add South West Africa to the rest of their territory. At the end of World War I, the newly formed League of Nations created a new category: the mandated territory. Each such territory was placed under the care of a more-developed country. Because South Africa was not yet a country but was a part of the British colonial system, the responsibility for governing South West Africa was given to Great Britain. But this was just a formality. Great Britain granted the actual administration of South West Africa to South Africa. South Africa was instructed to look after the material and moral well-being and development of its people.

The South African colonists set about to extend the same kind of rule over South West Africa as they had created at home in South Africa—reserving the best land for the whites and pushing the blacks into an inferior servant class. They also took a firm hold over Ovamboland, in the north, where nearly half the population lived. The Germans had never controlled this area.

Consolidated Diamond Mines have their headquarters in Oranjemund.

CONTROLLING THE WEALTH

South West Africa's main wealth at this time was in its vast supply of diamonds. The South Africans had carefully controlled the sale of their diamonds, making sure that prices remained stable no matter how many diamonds were mined. The German diamond merchants from South West Africa believed that the diamonds that were first found there in 1908 were limited in supply and would not last more than a generation. They were determined to finally earn some money from their investment in the territory. They flooded the market with diamonds. As a result, diamond prices dropped dramatically.

As soon as South West Africa came under South Africa's control in 1920, these diamond resources were carefully controlled. Only limited amounts were released onto the market, assuring firm and higher prices. Anglo-American, a South African company, gained control of the diamond mines in South West Africa and created Consolidated Diamond Mines (CDM).

A hotel near the mines used by white diamond merchants in South Africa.

By 1921 the South African settlers numbered eleven thousand, surpassing the eight thousand Germans in the territory. At this point, South Africa began to invest money in South West Africa, creating the basics of a modern society. Roads and housing were built, the rail system was extended, and supply lines for electricity and water were installed in urban commercial areas.

The South African colonists made these improvements only for the whites. They continued the restrictions on the Africans that had been started by the Germans. These restrictions were similar to those being established in South Africa at the same time. While the white South Africans did not want the blacks to live in the same areas, they needed their labor. To force the blacks to work for them, the whites collected taxes. They placed taxes on grazing lands, on huts, on dwellings, and more—all to be paid in cash. The Africans had no choice but to work on the white farms and in the white-run mining industry for cash.

MIGRANT LABOR

The work, however, was principally in areas where the blacks had been forced out in the 1890s. To solve this problem, the blacks were hired on contracts that usually lasted for a year. They were

Migrant workers eating in their cramped living quarters

transported to the mines, most of them in the south, where they stayed for a year while their families remained at home in the north.

This began the system of migrant labor that continues today. Migrant labor became the rule in South West Africa. This caused upheaval in the society. Men didn't see their families for the duration of their contracts. The people, either those at home or the migrants, were forced to live in reserves or designated territories. The hard work of planting crops for food was left to the women and old people. In many cases, the reserves did not even have the grazing areas needed to keep cattle alive.

During this time, the South African colonists passed an act that gave them complete control over the African chiefs and headmen in the reserves. The chiefs who didn't cooperate with the South Africans were dismissed. This left the Africans with no leaders they could trust.

FRAGILE ECONOMY

South West Africa's economy was dependent on just one commodity—diamonds. When the demand for diamonds fell in the late 1920s, as a result of a worldwide depression, production of diamonds in South West Africa was stopped. Sale of all diamonds was managed by a monopoly. If demand dropped, so did the supply. This kept prices stable. The diamond fields of South West Africa were kept idle until prices rose again. Even when production started again in the 1930s, it was still at a lower level than before. The income earned through taxes was very small. All of this limited South West Africa's economic growth. It was not until World War II in the 1940s that the economic engine got back on track.

During this time, South Africa had changed from a British Crown Colony to an independent nation within the British Commonwealth. In 1931, the British Parliament recognized South Africa's independence.

UNITED NATIONS ESTABLISHED

By the end of World War II, the League of Nations no longer existed. The United Nations (UN) was created to take its place. It was organized to sort out the many problems that remained at the end of the war. The colonies and territories that had been ruled as mandates under the League of Nations were to be handed over to the care of the United Nations. Although it was a charter member of the United Nations, South Africa refused to transfer its mandated territory. It was the only country to do so. Instead, at the first session of the United Nations General Assembly, in 1946,

Chief Hosea Kutako is called the father of nationalism.

it asked that South West Africa become a part of South Africa. South Africa claimed that most of South West Africa's people favored this plan. South Africa gave no explanation as to why the majority of people would favor being ruled by the white minority. But the people did not favor it. In 1946 Chief Hosea Kutako and the other chiefs joined together to send a petition to the United Nations opposing South Africa's move. Chief Kutako was a veteran of the 1904-1907 war and is considered the father of nationalism in Namibia.

The United Nations refused this request. The UN wanted more supervision over South West Africa, not less. The South Africans refused to comply with the United Nations demand. This set up a diplomatic battle that would rage for decades. South Africa made its request at a time when the economy had improved dramatically. It was ready to make use of the riches of South West Africa. South Africa wanted to keep control over the mineral resources in the region and to protect the prices as they had done in the 1930s.

IMPOSING APARTHEID

South Africa's ability to maintain control over South West Africa was strengthened after 1948, when the balance of power shifted from the English-speaking whites to the more conservative Afrikaners. The Afrikaners now had the strength of the law behind their desire to separate the races entirely. They called this policy *apartheid*, which means "separateness."

The Afrikaners applied apartheid to South Africa as well as to South West Africa. By 1949, South Africa had added six seats for representatives from South West Africa in its own Parliament, tightening its grip on the territory.

There was very little the Africans could do to protest. As was true from the time of the Herero-German War, superior weapons would always win the battle. The South Africans were now moving to separate the races. In one instance, they announced that a black township that was then part of Windhoek was going to be part of the whites' living area. The South African police were instructed to move the blacks out. On December 10, 1959, when the people protested this move, the police opened fire on the unarmed civilians. Thirteen civilians were killed and more than a hundred were wounded. The blacks were then moved to another area outside the city that they named *Katutura*, which means "we have no dwelling place."

By 1963 South West Africa had barely a half million people. Although only about 15 percent of the population was white, in 1964 South Africa moved ahead to divide the native peoples of South West Africa and to take away much of their land. They granted exclusive use of twice as much land to the whites as was given to the native people. White farmers raising cattle in the

In 1949 blacks were moved from Windhoek to Katutura *(above),
which means "we have no dwelling place."*

north central plateau and sheep in the south employed Africans.
Other than that, Africans were forced to live in reserves
designated by the South Africans. These reserves were further
divided into specific areas for each ethnic group, a move meant to
weaken the South West Africans' ability to form a unified
opposition to white rule.

SOUTH WEST AFRICANS REBEL

Organizing to protest against the harsh rules and laws of South
Africa's control was a slow and difficult process. In 1957, a labor
movement called the Ovamboland People's Organization (OPO)
was started by Herman Toivo ja Toivo to end the contract labor
system in South West Africa. OPO formed ties with the Herero
chief council representing the Herero people. The leaders of OPO,
including Sam Nujoma, were frequently arrested for their

activities. Many fled the territory and went into exile in countries all over the world, wherever they were welcomed and helped in their cause. In 1960 OPO became the South West Africa People's Organization (SWAPO), to show that it was working for all the people of the territory. Its stated aim was to overthrow South African rule in South West Africa.

One of the easiest places for South West African men to make plans was in the hostels where the contract workers were housed. Here, in these dormitories, the men had many hours to spend together after their work shifts ended. They had time to talk through their ideas and to organize the other workers.

THE UNITED NATIONS ENDS THE MANDATE

South Africa's policies toward South West Africa were continually disputed in the United Nations. In 1966 the General Assembly came to a long-delayed conclusion: that South Africa had violated the terms of its mandate by "failing to insure the material and moral well-being . . . of the indigenous inhabitants." As a result, the United Nations terminated the mandate and took direct responsibility for the territory. This was the only time in its history that the UN claimed a territory to be under its own protection.

In 1967 the UN Council for Namibia was created to administer South West Africa. A year later the council declared that the territory would be known as Namibia, in keeping with the wishes of the people. South Africa gradually withdrew from the various UN organizations and ignored these directives. The United Nations had little power to enforce its proclamations against South Africa, which was determined to go its own way. South

Africa even broke with Great Britain, dropping out of the British Commonwealth in 1961.

ARMED STRUGGLE BEGINS

While there was opposition to South Africa's rule through the years, the armed struggle did not begin until 1966, a year before the UN Council for Namibia was created. SWAPO had little in the way of material support. It began to conduct hit-and-run attacks from informal bases in northern Ovamboland where its people could blend in with the local people and be protected by them. This was the only part of the country where there was enough foliage to provide physical cover. Nevertheless, the SWAPO guerrilla fighters were quickly overwhelmed by the South Africa police. Those who were caught, including Herman Toivo ja Toivo who was head of SWAPO, were put on trial on charges of terrorism and sentenced to long prison terms.

SWAPO continued to recruit guerrilla fighters. It relied on any country that would supply financial help. South Africa moved to tighten its grip on Namibia, taking control of finances, business and industry, mining, and virtually all aspects of the territory's existence. It also increased its police presence in the northern parts of the territory, trying to stop SWAPO's raids.

In the early 1970s, SWAPO established bases for its guerrillas in the countries neighboring Namibia, particularly Zambia, whose long border with Namibia's Caprivi Strip made it an ideal site for such bases.

On December 12, 1973, the United Nations recognized SWAPO as the "sole and authentic representative of the people of Namibia."

Chapter 5

THE FIGHT FOR
INDEPENDENCE

LIVING IN EXILE

Tens of thousands of Namibians had to wage their fight for independence as exiles. Young people, some in their teens, left Namibia to take part in the long battle to free their country and their families from South African rule. One of these was Nangula Taapopi who left her home near the Angolan border when she was just fourteen. "I walked from my home to the SWAPO camps in Angola with some of my girl friends," she related. By the time she reached the SWAPO camps, she had covered about twenty-five miles (forty kilometers) of very dangerous territory. The bush was good cover for the South African soldiers on patrol and there was constant danger from the land mines that had been planted throughout the region. People such as Nangula were not even able to write letters home without putting their families in danger. "The South Africans would intercept the letters, steam them open, make a photocopy and then put them back in the mail. Then they would come to the parents' home and start asking questions about their children who were fighting for independence. If the parents said they didn't have such a child, they would show the copy of the letter. Some people were beaten. Some people were killed. And some people just disappeared—they were never heard from again."

UNITA forces in southern Angola

Nangula spent half her life in exile, first in Angola and then in Zambia, where she continued her education. Eventually, she went to college in East Germany (before it was united with West Germany), which was one of the countries supporting SWAPO's efforts to free its people.

SOUTH AFRICA HOLDS TIGHTLY

SWAPO's ability to fight for Namibia's freedom was almost entirely dependent on events outside its control. One of the principal events was the war for independence from Portugal being waged in neighboring Angola, to the north, on Namibia's doorstep. South Africa considered this border its last defense against a Communist-led state, providing an excuse for maintaining an armed presence in northern Namibia. South Africa and the United States actively supported UNITA, one of the three factions fighting for control of Angola after it became independent. South Africa didn't actually support UNITA's cause;

it was simply a convenient way to further its interest in suppressing the growing SWAPO resistance movement based in southern Angola.

When South Africa continued to ignore the demands of the UN that it release its illegal grip on Namibia, workers staged a massive and long strike starting at the end of 1971 and continuing into 1972. The workers effectively closed down Namibia's mining industries—and the wealth that made the country so attractive. The South Africans responded by declaring a state of emergency in Ovamboland where much of the guerrilla activity was taking place and where the strikers had been sent home.

WAR HEATS UP

South Africa continued its role in Angola's ongoing civil war even after Angola gained its independence on November 11, 1975. This was a particularly disturbing time in the region, with armed factions on all sides moving around the countryside. For the first time, SWAPO was able to move many of its armed men into southern Angola from their bases far to the east. There, they could mix with the Ovambo people who lived on both sides of the border that separates Angola and Namibia. South Africa's armed attacks against Angola were now being launched from bases across northern Namibia, stretching as far as the Caprivi Strip. Along this slender extension of Namibia's land that shares a long border with Zambia, SWAPO guerrilla fighters came into direct and frequent confrontation with the South African armed forces. While it kept up the fight to control Namibia, South Africa was under continued pressure from the United Nations to resolve the Namibian situation and allow the territory to gain its

Young South African cadets in training

independence. South Africa also faced a growing despair among its people as more and more of their young white men were drafted into the army to fight "on the border." Though the numbers of South Africans killed in the fight were small—one death in 1979, rising to sixty-one in 1981 and seventy-seven in 1982—they were bitterly resented, and the heaviest fighting was yet to come.

Young white men in South Africa, and their parents, began asking why they were being sent off to fight in Namibia; some left the country to avoid the draft. A popular song, "The Boy on the Border," described a girl's feeling for her soldier-boyfriend. The actual location of the soldiers on the Namibian front was a closely kept secret, and they were forbidden to include any such information in the letters they sent home.

SOUTH AFRICA STALLS

Meanwhile, South Africa continued to stall when faced with any serious plan that would lead Namibia to independence. But South Africa also began making some concessions to the

SWAPO
trainees

Namibian people. In 1978, the pass laws restricting movement
were repealed. The mixed marriage law, prohibiting whites from
marrying people of other racial groups, was revoked.

As South Africa's role in the Angola civil war expanded, so did
the number of its troops and its need to maintain control of
Namibia. By 1978 there were twenty thousand men stationed in
Namibia, and large parts of the north had been placed under
martial law. A year later the number of South African troops in
Namibia had risen to thirty thousand. SWAPO was using guerrilla
tactics against the modern South African army. SWAPO alone
could not win a war where South Africa had such a strong
military advantage.

South Africa's true intentions were dramatically revealed in
1977 when it created a "security zone" along the Angola border
by uprooting three thousand Ovambo who had been living there.
This no-man's land was about 0.6 mile (1 kilometer) wide and 280
miles (451 kilometers) long. A fence was built and alongside it
was placed a poisonous plant that caused extremely painful sores
if it was touched.

Trying to force some decisive action in 1977, a group of five nations—the United States, Canada, Great Britain, France, and West Germany—known as the Western contact group, was established to deal directly with South Africa on the Namibia issue. It was led by the American ambassador to the UN, Andrew Young, and his deputy, Donald McHenry. South African President John Vorster agreed to end apartheid in the territory and to allow elections in which SWAPO would take part.

TURNHALLE CONFERENCE

While all this was going on, the South African government attempted to head off the UN call for elections in Namibia. South Africa created its own body, called the Turnhalle Conference, in March 1977. This group was to draft a constitution for Namibia, leading to an interim government, and eventually to independence. But the Turnhalle group tried to set up a kind of independence built on racial separation. It would have allowed the whites control over their own communities, while giving the smaller black groups assurance that they would not be dominated by the Ovambo, who numbered nearly half the population.

South Africa invited to the conference delegates whom they considered "safe"—moderate leaders of Namibia's eleven "official" ethnic groups, including the whites. But no political parties were represented and SWAPO was not invited to take part. The results would hardly represent the Namibians' interests. While the Turnhalle delegates met over the next eighteen months, South Africa continued to interfere by setting up different levels of self-government for six of Namibia's ethnic groups.

*Donald McHenry, an American deputy ambassador to the United Nations (left)
and Justice Marthinus Steyn (right), the interim administrator-general of Namibia*

WALVIS BAY ANNEXED

In a move that indicated it expected to lose control of Namibia,
South Africa reannexed the enclave of Walvis Bay, Namibia's only
deep-water port, in September 1977. This confirmed the actual
legal status of the port, which had been claimed by South Africa
for nearly one hundred years. Through much of that time,
however, it had been administered from Windhoek. By making
the claim formally, South Africa gave itself an important
bargaining chip and continued to make life difficult for Namibia.

The UN General Assembly responded by recognizing Walvis
Bay as an integral part of Namibia. It condemned South Africa's
annexation as an act of colonial expansion. For South Africa,
Walvis Bay was a convenient port for shipping minerals mined in
Namibia as well as the site of one of its major military training
bases.

Also at this time, South Africa appointed Justice Marthinus
Steyn as administrator-general of Namibia. It was his job to
govern the territory while it was prepared for elections.

It appeared that progress was finally being made. The United Nations passed resolution 435, calling for the withdrawal of South Africa's administration and establishing terms for free and fair elections that would lead to full independence. A special UN representative, Martti Ahtisaari, was appointed to oversee the UN presence in Namibia during this period. The Security Council established the United Nations Transition Assistance Group (UNTAG). UN-supervised elections for a constituent assembly were supposed to take place by the end of 1978, but it was not to be.

SOUTH AFRICA HOLDS ELECTIONS

At the beginning of 1978, following SWAPO's demand that Walvis Bay be designated part of Namibia and its refusal to allow UN teams to monitor SWAPO bases in Angola, South Africa broke off the talks. President Vorster announced that South Africa would proceed with its own elections in Namibia. He declared that independence for Namibia would follow by the end of 1978. This may have been intended to limit the number of foreign observers, especially the UN team, in Namibia during this period. South Africa moved against SWAPO on all fronts and brazenly violated independent Angola's territory with an air strike on SWAPO's base at Cassinga, fully 155 miles (250 kilometers) north of the Namibian border.

On December 4-8, 1978, the South African-sponsored elections were held in Namibia, without UN supervision. These elections were boycotted by SWAPO and condemned by the UN. Reports of widespread intimidation were made, including people being forced to vote. Because the people were voting for the first time in

South African soldiers (left) and Dirk Mudge (right),
leader of the Democratic Turnhalle Alliance party

their lives, there was a great deal of excitement in Namibia, even though the elections were not a true representation of the people's wishes.

The business of Namibia continued to be run from South Africa. A degree of authority over local matters was granted to the ministerial council headed by a white politician, Dirk Mudge, who was leader of the Democratic Turnhalle Alliance party (DTA). Mudge would continue to play an important role in Namibian politics ten years later. South Africa continued to refuse to deal with SWAPO, which the UN had recognized as the only group that represented the Namibian people.

THE WAR SPREADS

A Namibian defense force was created during the 1970s, and by 1979 it had four battalions, including the Omega Battalion, made up of San. Although the San were originally brought in for their

*SWAPO guerrillas
practice using
their equipment.*

superb tracking ability, they also were being used as conventional
soldiers. But volunteers were not enough to fight the constantly
growing war. In 1980, the National Assembly in Namibia created
a military draft for all men, ages sixteen to twenty-five. In essence,
they were being asked to fight to delay their own freedom. Many
responded by fleeing the country and joining up with SWAPO in
neighboring Angola and Zambia. By 1986 it was estimated that as
many as sixty thousand Namibian refugees, including SWAPO
fighters, were living in those countries. The war raged on, in
Angola and in Namibia. SWAPO's attacks grew bolder as its
numbers increased. In a devastating move, SWAPO blew up the
power installation at Ruacana Falls, on the northern border. This
plant supplied much of the energy for Namibia. Its attackers also
moved south of the border, making life for the people of Namibia
more and more dangerous. Farmers feared for their families and
for their livestock, as SWAPO guerrillas penetrated deeper into the
countryside. Martial law was instituted over much of the country,
affecting 80 percent of the population. Ordinary life was becoming
more and more difficult.

In 1981 South African jets struck deep within Angola, attacking important military installations. At the same time, armored vehicles pursued SWAPO guerrillas based in Angola. The two wars—Angola's civil war and Namibia's war for independence— were interwoven. A solution for either one depended on solving both at the same time. This idea was proposed in 1982 by Chester Crocker, who was in charge of African affairs for the United States. He suggested linking Namibian independence to the withdrawal of Cuban troops from Angola.

South Africa was spending more of its budget fighting the war while investments were beginning to dry up. South Africa also feared that its investment in Namibia would be lost if Namibia gained its freedom under a hostile government. South Africa was particularly concerned about Namibia's enormous reserves of uranium, crucial to nuclear weapons production. It didn't want this mineral to fall into the "wrong" hands. Coupled with the ongoing cost of the war, South Africa's economy slowed to a crawl. Against the wishes of President Ronald Reagan, the U.S. Congress pushed through economic sanctions against South Africa.

SLOWLY MOVING FORWARD

Although there was a huge legacy of distrust on all sides of the issue, the process leading to independence was moving forward very slowly. By the end of 1983, South Africa's foreign minister, Roelof "Pik" Botha, was in contact with the secretary general of the United Nations, indicating his government would begin to withdraw its forces from southern Angola. South Africa released Herman Toivo ja Toivo on March 1, 1984, after he had served

Rallies to free Namibia were held in Katutura (left) and Windhoek (right).

sixteen years in prison. This popular figure had been replaced in SWAPO by Sam Nujoma who had fled Namibia many years before. Many felt Toivo ja Toivo's release was an effort to unseat Mr. Nujoma, who was seen as a more serious threat.

By the end of 1984, Angola had agreed that the masses of Cuban soldiers who were fighting on behalf of one of the factions in its civil war would begin to withdraw. This would mark a major shift in the balance of power in the region, since it was only with the help of the Cuban forces that Angola had been able to continue its civil war.

Although SWAPO's political activities were banned or suppressed through the years, the organization continued to have the support of the people, not only the Ovambo population but other groups as well. A curfew, passed in 1981, made it illegal to be outdoors from dusk to dawn, restricting the most ordinary kinds of everyday activity—even emergency visits to clinics. When a rally was permitted to be held in July 1986, more than thirteen thousand people gathered to show their support. It was a

Principals at the signing of the agreement for Namibian independence at the United Nations in 1989 are, left to right: South African Foreign Minister Roelof Botha, Secretary General Javier Perez de Cuellar, United States Secretary of State George Shultz, Angolan Foreign Minister Afonso Van Dunem, Angolan Vice Minister of Defense General Antonio dos Santos Frence, and Cuban Foreign Minister Isadoro Malmierca Peoli

considerable number in a country where few blacks have any means of transportation other than their feet.

By 1988, the number of refugees who had fled Namibia had grown and included sixty-nine thousand people who were living in refugee camps in Angola and five thousand more in Zambia.

RESOLUTION 435

Finally, on December 13, 1988, representatives of the Cuban, South African, and Angolan governments came together at the United States Mission to the UN in New York City to sign a tripartite agreement. This would lead to the total withdrawal of the Cuban troops from Angola and the implementation of the UN 435 plan for genuine elections leading to the independence of Namibia. The resolution that had been passed by the UN in 1978 took its first step to reality more than ten years later when Louis Pienaar, appointed by South Africa as Namibia's administrator-general, began the transition process to independence. Heading

Waiting to vote in Namibia's independence elections

the UNTAG team was Martti Ahtisaari, first appointed in 1978. Ahtisaari was from Finland, an especially appropriate choice for Namibia, which had received tremendous support from the Finnish people and from Finnish missionaries through the years.

The process got off to a shaky start with continued fighting across the border. SWAPO, in a deadly misjudgment, moved 1,200 guerrillas over to the Namibia side of the border as the cease-fire was to take effect. In the fighting that ensued, about 150 people were killed. For a brief period, it looked as if the whole peace process might be derailed. However, during the eleven months set aside for the transition, most of the plans were successful. South Africa withdraw its forces from Namibia, about half of the refugees returned home almost immediately under a general amnesty, and 98 percent of Namibia's registered voters eagerly turned out to elect members to a constituent assembly.

After waiting all their lives for a chance to determine their own future, people eagerly lined up in the intense heat and waited for hours, long before the polls were scheduled to open. Since about

President Sam Nujoma (right) swears in Prime Minister Hage Geingob (left).

60 percent of Namibia's people were illiterate, voters who could not sign their names were registered by their thumbprints. They chose candidates according to symbols that were familiar to them.

The elections, held from November 7 to 11, 1989, were the first in which all political parties, including SWAPO, were allowed to take part; SWAPO won more than half the vote, though not the two-thirds majority needed to act without the cooperation of the other parties. The DTA, still headed by Dirk Mudge, received one-quarter of the vote. Under the British Parliamentary system, this group is known as the "loyal opposition." Its members have proved to be valuable partners to SWAPO because of their practical experience in running the country during the ten years between the South African-sponsored elections and the genuine elections in 1989. Working together, the new assembly made use of a constitution that had been drafted in 1982. By February 9, 1990, a working constitution had been drafted and adopted. On March 21, 1990, Namibia became an independent country, with SWAPO leader Sam Nujoma as president.

Chapter 6

THE ECONOMY

WHERE TO BEGIN?

Namibia now faced the tremendous task of repairing the decades of damage done to its people by the South Africans. It had to find a way to overcome huge differences in education between blacks and whites. It had to integrate all the returning exiles, some of whom had been out of the country for as long as thirty years. It was a unique situation—exiled refugees returning to become leaders of the government. And it had to maintain the confidence of the business community to have the financial resources to carry out all these tasks and many more. With the country at peace Namibia could begin to deal with the tremendous job of dealing with the many victims of both the war and the seemingly endless time it had spent as a colony.

President Nujoma had spent thirty years in exile, working for Namibia's independence. Many feared he would immediately put into motion his Socialist ideas of redistributing land and wealth among all Namibians. Once in office, however, he quickly proved to be capable of recognizing the realities of the country he was elected to lead. Though Nujoma would like to shake off many of

Opposite page: A Namibian soldier reverently hoists the new flag, signaling the end of colonies in Africa. The unfurled flag (inset)

Seals off Cape Fria (left) and nesting flamingos (right)

Namibia's ties to South Africa as quickly as possible, Namibia remains heavily dependent on trade with South Africa. Many of its businesses are South-African owned and run.

POLITICS OF GEOGRAPHY

The territory of a country dictates the shape of its economy, and Namibia was born into the world community of nations with unique physical characteristics. Its only deep-water port, Walvis Bay, took some time in coming under Namibia's control. In August 1993, South Africa agreed to turn over control of the port to Namibia. Continued negotiating would likely finalize the transfer in 1994. One of the first signs of change was South Africa's decision to remove a battalion of its defense force from Walvis Bay. South Africa still claims nine islands that lie off the Namibian coast between Walvis Bay and the region of Luderitz. These remote islands are nesting grounds for seabirds and seals. The guano from the birds has traditionally been an important source of income.

The Caprivi Strip

One part of Namibia's sovereign territory that is not in dispute but is off-limits is a stretch of land that runs for hundreds of miles along the Atlantic Ocean coastline. It stretches from the South African border as far as Luderitz and as much as sixty miles (ninety-seven kilometers) inland. This is the property of CDM, owned by De Beers. On older maps of the country, this huge block of land, and another equally large area to the north, were marked off with dotted lines and the German word *sperrgebiet*, "forbidden territory." On new maps, the region is called Diamond Area 1 (Restricted Area). In reality, it remains off-limits, because De Beers guards its valuable diamond beach-mining operation very carefully. Armed guards patrol the shore, on the lookout for people coming in from the sea. Sensors planted throughout the forbidden zone guard against intruders arriving overland.

The third oddity about Namibia's geography is the Caprivi Strip. It seems to be trying to reach the other side of the African continent. Indeed, that was the original intention when this land was "given" to the German colonial government by Great Britain in exchange for the island of Zanzibar off the East African coast in

1890. This casual swapping of land was designed to allow Germany to link up its territories in southern Africa. The plan never succeeded, but it did put Namibia into physical contact with the Zambezi River. The strip is named for Chancellor Leo von Caprivi, who negotiated the Zanzibar Treaty of July 1, 1890, with Great Britain.

NATURAL RESOURCES

Namibia has the basic ingredients for a successful economy including substantial mineral wealth and a small population. The wealth, however, is concentrated in the hands of a few large companies. The local people gain from this wealth through the jobs offered at the mines and indirectly from the taxes paid to the nation by the mining firms. Most of the income, however, goes to the companies' owners. The taxes paid by the mining companies help support the government and the services provided to the people.

Namibia's mineral wealth is found in three areas of the country. Diamond mining is concentrated along the southern coast, with its base in the extreme southwestern corner of the country. In the middle of the country near the coast lies the huge uranium mine, and in the north is the mineral-rich area of Tsumeb, which yields many minerals, principally copper, lead, and silver. The nation's mining companies produce dozens of different types of minerals, most of them measured by tons of production. Nearly all of these mines were started more than fifty years ago. Mining conditions are among the most difficult encountered anywhere in the world because of the climate and the remote locations.

In addition to diamonds, Namibia's mining output includes

gold, lead, lithium, pyrite, silver, tin, copper, and zinc. Forty-four mines are being worked throughout the country today, the most valuable production being in diamonds. While mining operations today are very large-scale businesses, the people of Namibia were making use of some of these minerals long before the big companies arrived. Copper was being recovered from a surface deposit and smelted by the Ovambo back in the 1850s. It was used for tools, weapons, and jewelry. Copper was being mined at Tsumeb on a commercial basis by 1900.

While these mining operations support much of the economy, they are devastating to the environment. In the diamond mining area along the beach, tons of sand are removed to reach the diamond-bearing ore. Mountains of processed earth are left behind at every mine.

DIAMONDS

Diamonds occur in some of the harshest environments on earth and the deposits in Namibia more than live up to that description. The barren Namib Desert is a difficult place to work or live. The diamonds are found where the desert meets the ocean, buried beneath tons of sand. To get to them, the workers must move mountains of sand and then scoop out the diamond-bearing ore.

The diamond mine at Oranjemund was opened by CDM in 1928, with work taking place along the beaches and under the sea itself. The mine stretches northward along the beachfront from the mouth of the Orange River for some 62 miles (100 kilometers). Geologists believe the diamonds were formed inland and then swept along by the river until they reached the ocean. Over thousands of years, the diamonds were tumbled about by the

Workers scoop out diamond-bearing ore.

action of the waves until only the best diamonds were left. These
were buried in the sand, some close to the shore, some right on
shore. Some are found as deep as 328 feet (100 meters) beneath
the surface of the sea and as far as 12 to 25 miles (19 to 40
kilometers) off shore. The constant action of the waves, along with
the driving current, pushed the diamonds and deposited them all
along the shore for hundreds of miles.

Although diamond-mining began on the beaches, where the
first diamonds were found near Luderitz in 1908, it soon reached
into the sea itself. The richest diamond deposits are found in the
marine terraces, where they have been buried underneath tons of
earth. To mine the sea, the workers create dikes or walls of sand.
They use huge earth-moving equipment that rolls right along the
beach and builds up the dikes. Then the earth-moving equipment
scoops up tons of earth from an exposed area and rushes out of

the area to a flat surface where the diamond-bearing ore is transported to the sorting area.

Because the dikes are made of wet sand, they must be reinforced continually as the ocean is always trying to rush in over them. Pumps work around the clock to take water out of the mining area. The dike walls are sixty feet (eighteen meters) thick.

After vast amounts of sand, called overburden, are stripped away and piled into man-made dunes, the diamond-bearing ore is dug up and trucked to the recovery plants, where it is crushed in huge machines to release the diamonds. The diamonds are identified by X-ray machines. Diamonds have a quality called fluorescence. They give off a light that activates a jet of air. This blows the diamonds off the conveyor belt to a channel at the side. It's a rough-and-tumble beginning, but diamonds are the hardest mineral known and can take quite a lot of tough treatment.

No one lived in Oranjemund before the mining began, so everyone and everything in the town and mining area had to be brought in. The workers come from Ovamboland in the far north and work on six-month contracts, rarely going home to see their families. That is, most of the black workers have that arrangement. The white workers, and a limited number of black supervisors, live at the mine with their families.

Mining towns are the rule rather than the exception in Namibia. Many of the country's major towns and small cities were built by mining companies to work the minerals that had been found. The town of Oranjemund is an example of one such creation. Built and owned by CDM, it includes houses, schools, a hospital, restaurants, a movie house, and a supermarket. Even the neighboring farms were started by CDM to grow food for its employees.

A diamond mining area in South Africa near the Orange River

Because diamonds are so valuable—and so small—the security here is very tight. To enter the mine, a person must have permission and be escorted by a trusted employee. On the way out a security system randomly X-rays both visitors and miners. The idea is that because the workers never know when the machine will randomly select them, they can't take a chance on smuggling diamonds out. But in practice, miners do smuggle out diamonds, hoping that the machine won't choose them on that particular day. Millions of dollars worth of diamonds are smuggled out every year.

More than ten years ago, CDM showed its determination to be a progressive part of an independent Namibia. It moved the headquarters of the company from South Africa to Windhoek. It also opened a sorting house in Windhoek in 1988, where the newly mined diamonds are sorted according to size, color, and

Mining diamonds is laborious and dirty work.
One day's production (inset) is very profitable.

clarity. For more than seventy years CDM has been the single largest source of income for the government of Namibia, and it employs about sixty-five hundred people. CDM has opened three new diamond mines, including one in August 1991 at Elizabeth Bay, near Luderitz, where diamonds were first found in Namibia. This mine is expected to have a ten-year life span and to produce about 250,000 carats worth of small, gem-quality diamonds a year. Exploration of the seabed itself also is under way. There are diamond deposits well offshore, too far to be mined by creation of marine terraces like those at Oranjemund. These deposits will be worked by crews operating from ships.

URANIUM MINING

In the Rossing Uranium Mine, located in the Namib Desert about forty miles (sixty-four kilometers) from Swakopmund, the open-pit mine workings have created a huge hole in the earth.

The world's biggest open-cast uranium mine (left) is at Rossing. After the uranium is mined, it is processed at the metallurgical plant (right).

Though the company prides itself on the methods it uses to prevent dust and harmful gases from affecting the people working in the mine, the mine itself leaves a huge scar on the landscape. Eventually, the open pit will extend over two square miles (five square kilometers). There is an ever-present danger of radiation, although the company takes precautions to guard against anyone being harmed by this powerful mineral.

The mine is worked in terraces that are wide enough for trucks to be driven on them. Explosives are used to blast out the ore. The recovery process is similar to that of diamonds: the ore must be broken down by crushing it into small pieces for processing. The uranium produced at Rossing is used as fuel to generate electricity.

Unlike the diamond mines, where work has been going on for decades, the mine at Rossing is quite new. Although uranium was first discovered in the Namib in the 1920s, the mining site was developed starting in the 1960s. It did not come into full production until 1978. It is the largest-known uranium deposit in the world. Because it is so new, the company has never been part of the contract labor scene. All employees are housed within a short distance of the mine. The mine is expected to continue producing for at least another twenty-five years. The number of employees has been greatly reduced in recent years because of a worldwide overproduction of uranium. Rossing now employs between one thousand and fifteen hundred people.

Rossing prides itself on being a model employer and conducts many programs for its employees. The Rossing Foundation offers a number of educational programs for employees and their children, as well as for the community. These include scholarships to universities, literacy programs for adults, and farming instruction for small-scale farmers.

The third mining area in Namibia is known as Tsumeb. This mining group is owned by Gold Fields Namibia and operates both lead and copper mines. Like the other mining groups, Gold Fields has created mining towns complete with housing, schooling, and other services. It offers training programs for its employees and for the families of employees, and employs about four thousand people.

In the first years after independence, President Nujoma hoped for a great deal of foreign investment in all kinds of industries. A general recession and the needs of many other countries going through their own economic and political turmoil pushed Namibia's needs aside. Still, the skyline in Windhoek is dotted with new buildings and construction cranes, a sign of confidence on the part of the government and some South African businesspeople that the future of Namibia is a worthwhile investment.

Kavango are agricultural people. They pound millet for flour (left) and tend their gardens (right).

AGRICULTURE

Although Namibia is a vast nation with a small population, very little of its land is suitable for intensive farming. Much of the usable farmland is in the hands of large-scale commercial farms run by whites. Finding a way to redistribute Namibia's farmland while not scaring away the productive white farmers is likely to be one of the difficult, if not the most difficult, issues facing the government.

Communal farming occupies about 60 percent of the population. Another 12 percent are engaged in subsistence farming, just growing enough to feed their own families. Millet provides half of the staple food for the Africans. The rest of the diet includes maize (corn), used to make flour; groundnuts; sorghum; beans; and cassava.

DROUGHT

Even in the best of times, Namibia has a very dry climate, and irrigation is widely used. In 1992, a severe drought gripped much of the African continent, turning countries that were successful food producers into food importers. Namibia was not spared; 80 percent of its commercial maize crop was reported lost. All of Africa's southern and eastern regions, even countries that normally grew enough food to export, now had to import food. The drought also resulted in a major loss of farm animals as well, because both their grazing areas and their water supplies dried up. Three thousand tons of food left over from the Gulf War were donated to the Namibian government by the United States. The game animals in the parks suffered as well, and the government considered a plan in which the meat from these animals would be used to help feed the people. The drought was the most severe the country had faced in many years. This is an extreme example of the normal cycle of climatic conditions in Namibia.

CATTLE RANCHING

The commercial white-owned farms are mainly cattle ranches where beef cattle are raised for export, mainly to South Africa, with a small amount going to Europe. There are four meat-processing plants in the country, with two, in Windhoek and Okahandja, that meet the European Economic Community (EEC) requirements. The standards set by the EEC for cattle exports cannot be met by most of the African farmers because they don't have the great tracts of land needed to allow the cattle to graze and gain weight.

Beef production, including both commerical and communal farming, makes up about 87 percent of all agricultural income. In addition to cattle ranching, there are about three million sheep.

Domestic animals are raised for food (left). Pelts from the karakul sheep (right) are made into fine fur garments.

About seventy thousand are exported to South Africa on the hoof, which means Namibia does not even earn meat-processing income after their slaughter. While most of the beef cattle from Namibia are processed for use in regular meat products, such as steaks and hamburgers, a portion is turned into *biltong*, a kind of beef jerky that is very popular in southern Africa.

Before independence, food production in Namibia was directed almost entirely at supplying South Africa. A tomato farm and canning factory just north of the Orange River has been selling its production to South Africa. Much of the food needed in Namibia, such as grain and dairy products, must be imported.

KARAKUL SHEEP

A unique Namibian agricultural product is the fur of the karakul sheep. The sheep are well suited to normally dry areas. These animals have a tightly curled coat, which results in a very beautiful, valuable fur. While there is no domestic market for

A fisherman tends his nets.

karakul fur garments in Namibia because of the climate, tailors in Windhoek make karakul garments for sale to tourists. Most of the pelts are sold at fur auctions in Europe and are marketed under the brand name "Swakara," which is taken from the initials "SWA" for South West Africa and "kara" from karakul.

FISHING

Although the waters off Namibia were once full of fish, a lack of protection of those resources has left the country with severely overfished waters. A new protective zone was declared, the Exclusive Economic Zone (EEZ), stating that no unauthorized fishing boats may operate within two hundred nautical miles of the Namibian coast. Foreign boats found fishing within these limits have been seized and briefly held by the government. The government sets yearly quotas for catching pilchard, hake, horse mackerel, and crab. Local canneries process pilchards, fish meal, and fish oil for both domestic use and export.

This highway is typical of Namibia's excellent road system.
A red aloe plant thrives in the desert (left).

Chapter 7

TOURISM

The unique, rugged beauty of Namibia makes it a natural attraction for tourists. About 70 percent of the 100,000 visitors who come to Namibia each year are from South Africa. Namibia hopes to increase the numbers of visitors from abroad, particularly from the United States. The country appeals to German tourists, who find their language widely spoken. Namibia has opened a tourism promotion office in Frankfurt. Tourism is the most promising industry for Namibia, for it capitalizes on the country's natural resources. It offers great hope for future employment opportunities. Unlike mining, which uses up natural resources, tourism is based on visiting a resource without taking anything away except photographs and memories.

Namibia's excellent road system is a rarity in Africa. Visitors can drive to many sites on their own. There are only a few locations where one must travel with a guide or as part of an organized group. For adventuresome visitors Namibia's wildlife reserves offer unique habitats that reflect the country's unusual combination of climate and geography.

A variety of animals live in Etosha National Park. Clockwise from above are: warthogs, zebras and giraffes, gemsboks drinking water, and ostriches.

ETOSHA NATIONAL PARK

The best-known and most frequently visited reserve is Etosha National Park, in the north-central part of the country. This park is the size of the country of Switzerland and includes the Etosha Pan. A *pan* is a shallow depression of land that allows water to collect during the wet season. In Etosha, water seeps into the pan from drainage channels or accumulates during the brief, but very heavy, rains. The name *Etosha* means ''great white place of dry water,'' perfectly describing the look of the land. The salt residue gives the land a white color.

When water is plentiful, the animals spread out all over Etosha. When the water holes begin to dry up, the animals start to move toward the pan. The pan becomes smaller and smaller, and the

Black-faced impalas (top right) and a lioness trailed by her cubs

land grows parched and cracked. With the intense heat of the sun, it doesn't take long for the shallow water to evaporate. This constantly changing landscape makes it a challenge for visitors to locate the different species in the park.

Harsh conditions are part of the life cycle of the animals that live in Etosha, including rhinos. Even though the vegetation is usually very sparse, the park supports a population of ostriches, zebras, giraffes, and elephants. The grazing animals—eland, gemsbok, springbok, and impala—find a variety of grasses and bushes on which to feed, and the predators—the leopard, cheetah, and lion—find their food among the grass eaters. Several hundred bird species have been recorded at Etosha. During the rainy season, flamingos gather by the thousands.

Kaokoveld rhinos (left) and a desert elephant (right)

WILDLIFE

All wildlife follows this natural life cycle. In good seasons, when the rains come on time and there is plenty to eat and drink, the population increases. In dry seasons, fewer animal babies are born, and finding food and water becomes much more difficult for the adults. Dry conditions are the rule in Namibia, so the wildlife has adapted its habits to the lack of water.

Perhaps one of the strangest wildlife sites in Africa is the Kaokoveld. In the extreme northwest among the sand dunes, a small number of elephants and even some rhinos may be found. Both have adapted themselves to the extremely dry conditions. Unlike Etosha, where visitors may drive around on their own, tourists to the Kaokoveld must have a guide who is familiar with the terrain. It is considered too dangerous, because of the desert conditions and lack of roads, to permit visitors to come on their own.

The shoreline of Skeleton Coast and the remains of a nineteenth-century whaling pot (top left); Himba children (top right)

The people who live in this area, the Himba, are a vital part of the conservation effort. They are considered the guardians of the wildlife and help to protect the small but hardy herds of rhinos and elephants that have managed to survive in this dry climate. Scientists believe that the elephants, which are smaller than most in Africa, have adapted themselves to the extremely difficult conditions here and drink far less water than is normal. Instead of cooling themselves in ponds, these elephants protect their delicate skin from the harsh sun by covering it with a coating of fine dust.

SKELETON COAST PARK

Just to the south of the Kaokoveld, a stretch of shoreline has been designated Skeleton Coast Park, a region of sand dunes and

Skeleton
Coast
Park

Windhoek

Seals at Cape Cross Seal Reserve

rugged terrain. Visitors who like fishing or just watching the seals and dolphins playing in the surf find this remote park a delightful place to visit. Hikers who want to walk the Ugab River Hiking Trail may join the two-day guided hikes. Otherwise, access is very limited, since traveling in this region is both difficult and dangerous. The park itself, running along the Atlantic Ocean, is about 311 miles (500 kilometers) long and only about 25 miles (40 kilometers) wide. Seals and dolphins may be seen splashing about in the surf.

Many other game reserves have been established in Namibia, some having just one species. One of the best seal viewing areas is at Cape Cross Seal Reserve, about 80 miles (129 kilometers) north of Swakopmund, where a seal colony makes its home. About 80,000 to 100,000 seals gather here to feed and breed, undisturbed by visitors. Like most of Nambia's wildlife reserves, Cape Cross is difficult to get to, which makes it likely that the seals will be left in peace to enjoy their special place along this wild coast.

Flamingos (left) and cormorants (right)

At Walvis Bay, where whaling boats used to stop on their way around the Cape of Good Hope, visitors may see large numbers of pelicans, flamingos, and a variety of smaller seabirds. A bird sanctuary here attracts many species of African birds, including geese, cranes, and cormorants. The wetlands of Walvis Bay make it an ideal breeding ground for huge numbers of flamingos. They migrate in and out of the region each year.

LIFE IN THE NAMIB

Life in the Namib is a matter of adapting to the conditions. Several small creatures, including the darkling beetle, survive by taking advantage of the fog that rolls in most mornings. They climb to the very top of the dunes, and wait, head down, for the fog. As the fog rolls by, drops of moisture form on their bodies and trickle into their mouths. The Namib gecko manages to hold onto the slippery surface of the dunes by webbing grown between

77

The welwitschia mirabilis *is a plant that is well adapted to the desert.*

its toes. One type of gecko keeps changing alternate front and back legs to keep its feet from burning on the hot sand.

PLANT LIFE

Like everything else in Namibia, the plant life that survives must adapt to the desert climate. One such survivor is the *welwitschia mirabilis*, a plant that looks dead even when it is at its best. The *welwitschia* depends on the fog for its life. On the surface, it appears to be an immense turnip, with two tough leaves. The leaves grow very long and lie on top of the sand. The life of the plant is below the surface, where the roots run deep into the ground to seek moisture. When the fog rolls in, the long flat leaves provide a large surface to collect the life-giving moisture. The moisture is absorbed into the leaves. Some of these

Bottle tree (above) and the quiver tree (right)

plants are more than a thousand years old. They lie out in the desert undisturbed by wildlife or people.

Desert trees typically have very thick trunks and spindly branches, and in place of leaves often have thorns. Leaves demand much more water than such plants will ever know. Instead, they put all their energy into conserving water in the trunk. The San traditionally made extensive use of the plants and trees that live in their areas. The bottle tree provided a poison used on their arrows that enabled them to hunt large game animals. Another tree, whose name is the *kokerboom*, but which is known as the "quiver" tree, provided wood used for the arrows. Many plants in Namibia have evolved a life cycle that allows them to exist in a dormant state until an occasional rainfall brings them to life. Then, the seeds that have been waiting spring into life. The plants quickly flower and are pollinated by passing insects. This provides the seeds for the next life cycle. Years may pass in between.

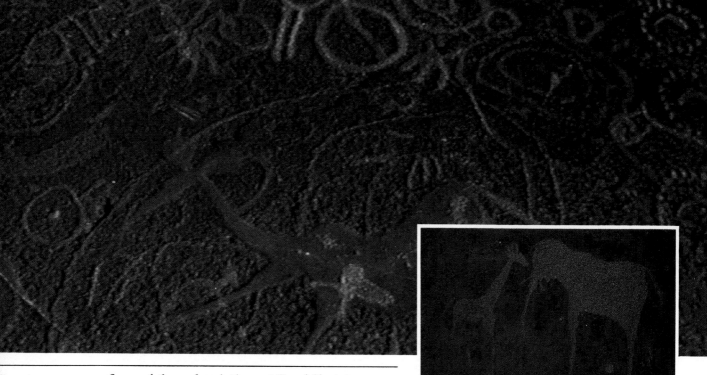

Some of the rock paintings at Twyfelfontein are easy to interpret, while others are more mysterious.

ROCK PAINTINGS

Proof that the San have been present in Namibia for many centuries may be seen in paintings they created on the sides of the rocks and mountains. Their pictures of giraffes and other animals were perfectly preserved by the hot, dry air and remain undisturbed.

The main sites of the rock paintings are at Ameib and at *Twyfelfontein*, which means "doubtful spring" in Afrikaans. Both sites are in the western part of the country near Brandberg. At Twyfelfontein there are more than twenty-five hundred etchings and paintings that may be visited. The paintings are located on a private farm owned by a Namibian farmer, Elias Aro Xoagub. He has worked with the ministry of wildlife conservation to maintain the paintings and to help the local people earn money by selling their crafts to the tourists who visit the site.

Fish River Canyon

FISH RIVER CANYON

In the south, not far from the Orange River, is one of Namibia's natural wonders, the Fish River Canyon. This huge canyon is similar in appearance to the Grand Canyon in the United States, and features a sharp drop and rough walls that were carved out by a river. It measures 100 miles (161 kilometers) long, 17 miles (27 kilometers) wide, and nearly 1,804 feet (550 meters) deep. Within the canyon lives a variety of wildlife, including mountain zebras, kudus, baboons, and leopards. Visitors may hike into the canyon only during certain months of the year when the danger from flash floods is past. At the southern end of the trail are the Ai-Ais Hot Springs.

HUNTING

Namibia is one of the few countries in Africa where hunting is allowed. It is strictly controlled and permitted only in designated areas, including private farms and on communally owned lands. No hunting is permitted anywhere in the wildlife preserves. Each visitor who wishes to hunt must follow the rules, which designate the kinds of animals that may be hunted, the kinds of weapons that may be used, and even the way the hunt is conducted.

Such strict controls often help a country conserve its wildlife. Poachers without any concern for preserving the species are less likely to operate in a country where they know there are professional hunting guides, armed with weapons, out in the bush. In some countries of East Africa, after hunting was banned, the poachers moved in and virtually finished off the rhino population. They were well on their way to doing the same with the elephants before a worldwide ban on ivory was enacted. Even in Namibia, poachers have been a problem and some reports have indicated that as few as sixty rhino may be left. Another rare species, the sable antelope, may be found in Mahango National Park. These species, of course, may not be hunted.

For hunters, and for conservationists, the mature male is the ideal example of the species. In many species, the mature male has the most beautiful horns, so it appeals to the hunter who wants to bring home a "trophy." In terms of conservation, it is also the best animal to shoot because its loss does not disrupt the lives of the mother and her young, nor does it take away younger males who are needed for future breeding. In Namibia, mature males are the only animals that hunters are permitted to shoot.

Among the species hunters may go after are a variety of African

Wolfgang Delfs (left) supplies wild animals to parks and zoos, such as this panther (right).

antelope, ranging in size from the eland, kudu, and gemsbok to the tiny duiker. Hunters usually go out with hunting guides who have ranch land or farmland that has wildlife living on it. Many such ranchers and game farmers make their land available to hunters. The fees they earn from the hunters are quite high, and this often enables them to continue to stock their land with wildlife. Some see the hunting aspect as a necessary evil. Though they may not understand why someone would want to shoot an animal for sport, they recognize that sometimes the balance of animals on the land can become upset. Allowing hunters on their land to shoot these animals is a way to restore that balance.

CATCHING WILD ANIMALS

Wolfgang Delfs, a professional game catcher, has been supplying wild animals to safari parks and zoos for more than thirty years. He came to Namibia from Germany in 1952. In 1961

After a temporary corral is built (left), the animals are herded into the area (inset).

Delfs began to create a private game reserve of wild animals on his twenty-thousand-acre (eighty-one-hundred-hectare) ranch, in the north near the urban center of *Otjiwarongo*, which means "the beautiful place." It was given that name because there are natural springs nearby. In the beginning, Delfs brought animals to his land and allowed them to breed. Some species were already there. In all, he has twenty-five species, numbering several thousand animals. In this way he created his own supply of wildlife. It took years before he was able to establish a balance between the prey and predator animals.

When Delfs gets an order from a safari park, it's like a shopping list of wildlife: they want so many of this animal and so many of that. Delfs and his workers then go out and catch the animals, using a technique that involves herding the animals into a temporary corral. The "walls" are actually made of brown or black plastic that has been stretched out and attached to the trees. When the animals run into the corral, the plastic is then quickly

Once the animal is in the corral, it is chased to a waiting truck.

stretched across the opening and the corral is secure. The animals just see a wall. They don't know it is only made of plastic and so they don't try to escape. They are herded into a smaller area and then up a ramp into a waiting truck. This is a much more efficient method than the old way of chasing an animal until one could fire an anesthetic dart into it, waiting for it to fall asleep, and then lifting it into a vehicle. Even working on his own land, however, catching is still not a sure thing for Delfs. The wildlife is so widely dispersed, he has to go searching for it.

After the animals are in the truck, they're taken to a special holding area where they have a chance to calm down, get used to their surroundings, and begin to eat the food that's provided. Later, they'll be taken to a quarantine station and held there before being sent out. Each country has different requirements about how long and where animals must be held in isolation to be sure they are free of disease before they may be admitted. The animals are sent by ship in huge crates that allow them to move around during the long journey.

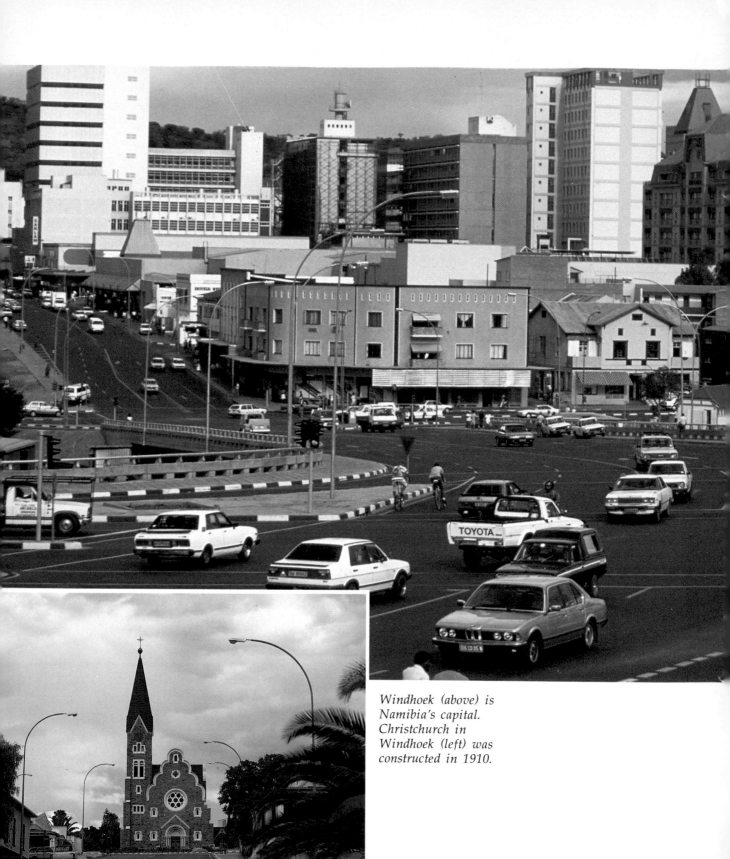

Windhoek (above) is Namibia's capital. Christchurch in Windhoek (left) was constructed in 1910.

Chapter 8

THE CITIES

Although Namibia's cities are small, they have recently experienced a sudden spurt in population. This is a result of the return of thousands of people who had fled the country during the war for independence. Many who once lived in the rural areas have moved into the cities because their homes were destroyed and their families disrupted. They are now seeking assistance in the cities. The urban populations have grown quickly, with many people living in makeshift housing while they try to find work.

WINDHOEK

Windhoek, the capital city, is situated in the center of the country. Although located at nearly the highest point in the country, it is sheltered by mountains. The site was a Herero cattle post until a group of Nama settled there in 1840.

Windhoek has a German flavor to it. Many of the old buildings are German in design, a reminder of the country's colonial past. This is also true of the street names which refer to well-known historical German figures such as Brahms and the Brothers Grimm, plus other Germans who played a role in Namibia's past,

Windhoek (above) was founded in 1890. The old Turnhalle building (above right) is still in use. A king and queen are part of a German carnival celebration (right). A fashion show (below)

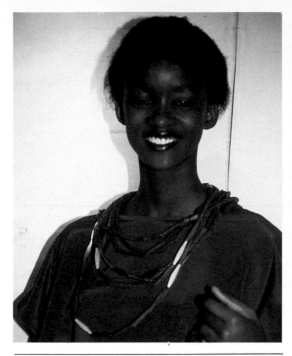

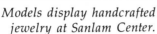
*Models display handcrafted
jewelry at Sanlam Center.*

such as Leutwein and Bismarck. The first European-style city
began in 1890 when a German garrison was relocated there from
Swakopmund.

Today, Windhoek is a modern city with first-class hotels and
shops offering such local products as karakul fur, gemstone
specimens, and jewelry set with tourmalines, tigereye, and other
gems mined in Namibia. Most of the shopkeepers speak German
and one of the popular restaurants is a German pub. The larger
shops are usually part of South African chains. The town
celebrates German holidays with parades on Independence
Avenue, formerly known as Kaiser Street, with people dressed in
German costumes. Modern fashion shows and fun fests are held
near the shopping center at Sanlam Center, named for a big
insurance company. A new National Crafts Center, the University
of Namibia, and a new Parliament are among the buildings that
have sprung up since independence. The old Turnhalle building is

Above: A thank you to the United Nations was painted by Namibian children. Below: a crafts show in a shopping center (left) and the Parliament building (right) in Windhoek

Walvis Bay is Namibia's only deep-water port.

still in use. A brightly painted mural, the work of Namibian children, is a thank you to the United Nations for helping the country achieve its independence.

Although segregation is no longer officially practiced in Namibia, most blacks continue to live in the housing that is available to them at the lowest income levels. Katutura is still the major living area for urban Africans.

WALVIS BAY

This fine natural harbor was first visited by American whaling boats in 1784. The name *Walvis* means "whale." The port was annexed by the United Kingdom in 1878 and made part of Cape Colony (South Africa) in 1884. Even after Germany claimed most of the territory that would become Namibia, the port of Walvis Bay remained in British and South African control. Walvis Bay is returning to Namibian control. When the changeover is complete, the port, the fishing industry, and the income earned from it will be an important part of the Namibian economy.

Luderitz is a quiet town on the southern coast. It has a natural harbor (inset) but cannot handle large ships.

KEETMANSHOOP

In the south is Keetmanshoop, founded in 1860. The name means "Keetman's hope." It is a major rail center where rail lines connecting different parts of the country converge. The town is the center of the karakul fur business. One of the landmark buildings is the Rhenish Mission church built in 1895.

LUDERITZ

Luderitz is Namibia's other natural harbor, although it cannot handle large ships and is of limited use. The site was first reached in 1486 by the Portuguese navigator Bartholomew Diaz, who called it Angra Pequena, but it is named for Adolf Luderitz who established a trading station there in 1883. Situated along the southern part of the coast, it was once the center of the fishing

Swakopmund (left) and the ghost town of Kolmanskop (above)

industry. Diamond mines located nearby made it a boom town, but when the diamond mines were abandoned the town nearly disappeared. It is a quiet place to visit and offers a natural breeding ground for fish and a sanctuary for bird life. Just outside the town lie the remains of Kolmanskop. It has turned into a kind of living ghost town, with sand dunes slowly creeping into the homes that were abandoned when the diamond mines closed.

SWAKOPMUND

Situated on the coast just north of Walvis Bay, Swakopmund was an important harbor when Walvis Bay was under the control of the British. Today it is a popular beach resort favored by white visitors, retaining the German look of its early twentieth-century architecture. Among the town's industries are a brewery, a tannery, and a salt mine. Namibia's beer, brewed under a number of names, is considered by many to be the best in Africa.

Chapter 9

EVERYDAY LIFE

DIVERSE PEOPLE

Distinct cultures are well established in various parts of the country, principally the Ovambo, Himba, Herero, San, and Baster. In the rural areas, traditional ways are still an important part of everyday life. While English has been designated the official language of Namibia, most people outside the urban areas speak their own languages.

OVAMBO

The Ovambo have always been the largest ethnic group in Namibia, accounting for nearly half the total population. They live in the northernmost part of the country, as well as in the southern part of Angola, along both shores of the Kunene River. The Ovambo lived in this region long before there was a border dividing the land into two countries. It is believed that the Ovambo migrated into the region from the central lake district of Africa. They are an agricultural people who settled on land that was suitable for farming. Their *kraals*, or "family compounds," are

Young Ovambo women fishing in the Kunene River (left) and a Herero village (right)

built like mazes, with many twists and turns for protection. Their stable settlements made them attractive candidates as laborers for the industries and factories of South West Africa. Virtually all of the people working at the mining towns of Tsumeb and Oranjemund are Ovambo.

HERERO

The Herero who live in Namibia today have survived many hardships. They were reduced to barely fifteen thousand people after the German massacres early in the century. The Herero lived in the central plateau for hundreds of years with the Damara and Nama to the south until the 1904-1907 war, when they were removed by force to the northeast near the Kalahari, an area marked by a hot and dry climate where little vegetation grows. It is a harsh existence for the people and their livestock.

Herero women devised a unique style of Victorian dress patterned after the clothing of the wives of the German

Herero women wear gowns and headdresses patterned after the outfits worn by the wives of the German missionaries.

missionaries at the end of the nineteenth century. They still wear this costume, a long dress with many skirts beneath it and a distinctive and matching headdress, often in the shape of a pillow.

The Herero perform a ritual known as "The Holy Fire of the Herero." A fire is lit each sunset and sunrise, but only by someone who is considered to possess special spiritual powers. This fire is thought to communicate with the Herero's ancestors and with God. The people who are singled out for this honor are often recognized when they are still very young. The fire is made only from certain kinds of wood.

In the heart of Hereroland, near the town of Otjiwarongo, the Herero fought the devastating Battle of Hamakari against the Germans on August 26, 1904. Each year on that day, the battle is commemorated as Heroes Day and marked here, on the plains below the Waterberg Plateau.

A Himba cattle breeder wears leather garments and decorates his body with ocher.

HIMBA

The Himba, a very small subgroup of the Herero, live in Kaokoland, in one of the most remote and difficult parts of Namibia. The Himba are cattle breeders who traditionally lived a seminomadic life, often on the move looking for grazing and water. They are well adapted to the brutal climate and living conditions. After the drought of the 1980s took about 90 percent of their vast herds, they were forced to adopt a completely new way of life. Although some have rebuilt their herds, many have drifted away from the cattle-based culture of their ancestors.

Traditional Himba are easily recognized by their dress and ornamentation. They wear leather garments made from the skin of their livestock and decorate themselves with ocher, which gives their skin a reddish color. By the time the first European explorers reached this part of the coast, four hundred years ago, the Himba were well established in the area and had built up huge herds.

BASTERS

A group of mixed-race people who came to Namibia from Cape Colony in the late 1860s are known as Basters, or Rehobothers. In 1870 their leader obtained the town of Rehoboth, about 53 miles (85 kilometers) south of Windhoek, from the Nama and Herero chiefs.

SAN

Throughout their history, the peaceful San of Namibia have retreated when their territory has been invaded by more aggressive people. From the moment the first white settlers arrived in the Cape district of South Africa and began moving around the territory, the San lost ground. They kept moving into the less habitable parts of the territory. Finally, they were left with areas that no other people could live in. By the time the Germans had finished their occupation, the San were left with the forbidding Kalahari as their home. They were able to survive there because of their remarkable ability to make use of the land, the plants they found, and the animals they encountered in ways unknown to others. They also depended on sharing everything they had with other San, but still their lives were very difficult. There was no margin of safety. They lived in small groups, several families to a group, constantly on the move as they searched for food.

The nomadic life of the San virtually came to an end when the South Africa government decided that part of the Caprivi Strip was to be turned into "homelands" for the San. This was the same technique that South Africa was using to separate the various

The San people live in the Caprivi Strip.

peoples in its own territory. This deprived the San of much of their territory and made it impossible for them to continue their way of life as hunters and gatherers, living off the land. Much of the land that was taken from the San was turned into game reserves.

It would have been possible for the San to continue to live on the land even after it was designated as a game reserve, since they have always lived in harmony with the land and the animals and have used very few animals for food. But the San represented a "primitive" way of life to the ruling South Africans, who did not want the San to come in contact with the tourists who would be visiting the game reserves.

OMEGA BATTALION

During the war for Namibian independence, the life of the San changed most dramatically. Many were pressured into joining the South African Defense Force (SADF) in its fight against SWAPO.

Soldiers from the Omega Battalion

The San became the Omega Battalion and were used as trackers,
following the enemy SWAPO soldiers into the bush. Their way of
life changed completely; they earned cash money, wore uniforms,
and were given military rankings. When the war was over, and
the army no longer needed the San, they lost their new way of life
yet were unable to go back to the old ways. The San feared what
might lie in store for them when the new SWAPO-ruled
government, which they had just been fighting, took over. So
nearly the entire Omega Battalion, eight hundred trackers and
soldiers, plus their families—four thousand people in all—were
moved to an army camp near Kimberley in South Africa. There,
they try to earn a living by traditional crafts, making and selling
implements such as knives and bows and arrows.

NAMA

The Nama, also known as Khoikhoi, are similar to the San in
their physical appearance. Slight of height, with light tan-colored
skin, they have prominent cheekbones and distinctive tightly

Nama people

curled hair. Their speech is marked by clicking sounds. There are several different clans within the Khoikhoi, one of the best known being the Witboois. They were driven out of the Cape area of South Africa when the Europeans first arrived in the seventeenth century. The Khoikhoi keep cattle but also live as hunter-gatherers. Traditionally they built distinctive beehive-shaped shelters of reeds over a wooden frame.

DAMARA

The Damara, sometimes called the Berg-Damara, were among the earliest inhabitants of Namibia who lived as hunter-gatherers. *Berg* means "mountain" in German, and remote mountain ranges were usually their homes. The Damara were easily conquered people who had no central leadership to guide and protect them. As a result, they were taken as slaves by the Nama and by the Herero. Their own ancient language was lost when they became enslaved and they now speak a language similar to that of the Nama.

Kavango children (left) and modern paintings at the Sanlam Center (right)

KAVANGO

The Kavango are an agricultural people who migrated into the region along with other peoples from central and eastern Africa. They live along the Kavango River, which is named for them. There are an estimated sixty-five thousand to seventy thousand Kavango living in Namibia.

CRAFTS

Traditional crafts are part of everyday life for many people in Namibia, even though they may no longer live a traditional life. Basket weaving and pottery are crafts practiced by many different groups. These objects are not only useful to the people who make them, they also offer a way for people to earn money by selling their products at exhibitions in various parts of the country. The Opuwo Art Project, funded by the United Nations Development Program and the New Zealand High Commission, created a place where the Himba could learn to make their traditional objects

Left: A Himba couple wear some of their crafts.
Right: Part of a crafts display at Sanlam Center

more appealing to outsiders. This would enable them to earn a
cash income. The American Embassy in Windhoek presented
some of the work at a special show, and a Himba couple, in
traditional costume, came from their *onganda*, "homestead" to
display their crafts, to explain them, and to sell their work. A
permanent home for crafts is found at the new National Crafts
Center in Windhoek.

MODERN CULTURE

Modern culture in Namibia includes the National Theater of
Namibia, a group that performs plays that depict village life as
well as contemporary ideas. They bring important ideas, such as
conservation, to life through their plays, helping people make the
transition to a more modern way of life.

Immediately after independence, Namibia adopted a new,
English-language national anthem. The words describe the
struggles the people faced along the road to becoming a nation. At

Enjando *was a weekend celebration of independence. It ended with a candlelight ceremony in which children sang the new anthem.*

the close of *Enjando*, a weekend celebration of the country's independence, children sang the new anthem at a candlelit ceremony.

EDUCATION

One of the most difficult problems facing Namibia is the education of its people, not just the children, but young adults and grown-ups as well. The system left in place by South Africa was not aimed at educating the youth of an independent country. Now, the unequal education that favored whites is being replaced by one that tries to offer all students a chance at a good education.

In addition, Namibia has chosen English as the official language of the country to unite all the different people and to be able to make its way in the modern world. Simply naming English as the official language does not mean that most of the people know how to speak it. This is another task for Namibia.

Thousands of young people, who went into exile during the years that Namibia was fighting for independence, were educated in different countries, in different languages, often with ideas that they discover are not very useful today. The collapse of communism in the former Soviet Union and the other Eastern European countries and the failures of the idea of central planning have left many unprepared.

Some returning exiles have discovered that the education they earned in Eastern European countries often has not provided them with usable skills or knowledge that is suitable for jobs in Namibia. A program and money to fund it are needed to help in their retraining. Many also have to learn English.

Adult literacy is another area that must be addressed. Only about 40 percent of adults in Namibia can read and write—in any language. This makes it much more difficult to improve their way of life. For the majority who live in rural areas, it prevents them from learning about better farming techniques and ways to conserve water and soil. For those who want to work in the mining industry, or in any of Namibia's factories, it means being limited to low-end jobs.

COMPULSORY SCHOOLING

Since independence, education has been made free and compulsory up to the age of sixteen. This is the ideal that Namibia strives to meet. However, because parents must buy uniforms for their children, and because there aren't enough teachers available, many children receive only a few years of education, rarely going past the sixth grade. There are about 350,000 students in school, at all levels, in Namibia.

Children in the rural areas are taught in their own language for the first six years and take English as a subject. This is reversed when students continue to the higher grades. Then they are taught all subjects, except their own language, in English. Namibia has been helped by volunteers from other English-speaking countries.

HEALTH

The system of health care that Namibia inherited after independence was very limited. There were only two main hospitals, one in Windhoek and one in Oshakati in the north. But most people live far from these hospitals. A major effort is underway to set up small clinics all over the north that can offer basic care, usually on an emergency basis. These clinics, some of them mobile, are allied with regional and district hospitals where more complicated procedures can be carried out. Improved health care is one of the many priorities of the government.

SPORTS

Shortly after gaining independence, one of Namibia's first requests was to be granted a berth at the 1992 Summer Olympics in Barcelona, Spain. The request was granted and a team of runners, swimmers, and boxers proudly represented their country along with the other nations of the world. One of the leading runners from Namibia, called by some Africa's fastest man, is Frankie Fredericks, who was born in the black township of Katutura. He has, on occasion, beaten world-class athletes including Carl Lewis and Ben Johnson. He runs sprints—200 meters and 100 meters. In 1992, at Barcelona, he finished second in both the 100 meter and the 200 meter track and field events and was awarded two silver medals.

Fredericks, like many young boys in Namibia, loved to play soccer, but he gave it up when he discovered he could run. After working at Rossing Uranium, where he also ran for the company's sports team, Fredericks was sent to a university in the United States.

Soccer, known as football, is considered the national sport. Clubs are organized into a league, with different sections of the country competing against each other. They also field a team that plays the best teams from other African countries in the African Cup competition.

ROAD RALLY

Also in 1992, the Paris-Cape Town rally, although only a spectator sport, and an odd one at that, roared through Namibia as it neared the end of its 7,717-mile (12,419-kilometer) journey. In the past, these high-speed racing cars, known as Formula 1 automobiles, traveled only as far as Dakar, Senegal. But for the first time the race that ended January 16, 1992 was extended all the way down to the end of the continent. The longer route was possible because the wars fought over Angola and Namibia had ended. The race was routed away from the main roads to avoid accidents and some wondered about the environmental damage. Still, the Namibian government looked upon this event as a major boost to the country's economy and another sign for Namibians that their country is really joining in the activities of the rest of the world, even if some of them are rather frivolous.

A worker marks a stretch of a newly-paved street in Windhoek

Chapter 10

INDEPENDENT NAMIBIA

TRANSPORTATION

For a country with fewer than two million people, Namibia has an extremely well-developed system of roads and railroads. There are more than 25,983 miles (41,815 kilometers) of roads. While most are not paved, the lack of rainfall means they don't suffer from rutting and potholes.

Namibia has an extensive rail system, largely a result of the mining industry's needs as well as South Africa's interest in connecting its cities with the produce of Namibia. There are some 2,000 miles (3,218 kilometers) of railroads. Lines connect Namibia with South Africa and run northward as far as Tsumeb and Grootfontein. A branch runs westward from Windhoek to the coast, linking up Swakopmund and Walvis Bay. Another coastal spur connects the main north-south line to Luderitz.

AIR NAMIBIA

A growing number of international airlines now fly to Windhoek, arriving from other African cities as well as from major European cities. Namibia boasts its own domestic airline called Air Namibia. It links cities within the country, making it much easier for travelers and businesspeople to cover the huge distances. Airports serve Oranjemund in the south, and Oshakati,

Runtu, and Katima Mulilo in the Caprivi Strip in the extreme
north. Air Namibia flies to major cities in neighboring African
countries and also to Frankfurt, Germany.

COMMUNICATION

Namibia enjoys a lively television and radio network presented
by the Namibian Broadcasting Corporation (known as NBC). The
television service broadcasts only during evening hours, a total of
forty-nine hours a week, on a single channel. Most of these
programs are from Great Britain and the United States.
International news comes from many sources, including CNN.
The radio network broadcasts in twelve languages for a total of
eighty-five hours a week. It also offers twelve hours of English-
language programming each day, including news and music.
Radio programs include instruction in English, health care, and
agriculture.

Namibia has a large number of daily newspapers for a country
with such a small population, and such a small percentage who
can read. Windhoek is dotted with bookstores that offer books in
English, German, and Afrikaans.

THE TASKS OF INDEPENDENCE

After the first excitement of independence, Namibia found it
was left nearly alone to face an astonishing array of tasks. All
races are now officially equal, but they come together on a playing
field that is far from level. Among the many legacies left behind
by South Africa is a bureaucracy that employs one-fourth of all
the working people in the country. Yet, to keep peace, Namibia

has agreed not to reduce this burdensome overemployment.

Although apartheid has ended in Namibia, the structure created to run it remains in place. To control the people, South Africa divided the Namibians into eleven ethnic groups (although all whites—Germans, Afrikaners, British—were counted as one group). A separate and costly bureaucracy was created for each group. The result was a tremendous number of office workers in relation to the population. South Africa, which treated Namibia as a colony and in the process helped to support the economy, pulled out its financial support entirely when Namibia gained independence. This has made it even more difficult for the country to pay its way in the world. Unemployment, which was high before independence, had become much higher with the return of the former exiles. Countries that Namibia counted on to invest in new businesses held back, partly because of a recession that affected much of the world and partly because of urgent needs in many other parts of the world. But Namibia must try to satisfy its own urgent needs such as education, improved health services, housing, and absorption of the returned exiles. In Namibia, nearly all the usable farmland is in the hands of whites. Finding a way to redistribute Namibia's farmland that does not scare away the productive farmers is likely to be one of the most frustrating issues for the average Namibian citizen.

NAMIBIA AND SOUTH AFRICA

South Africa's influence over Namibia can be felt in almost every aspect of life. It will take many years before the inequality built into the Namibian economy begins to fade. It will also take many years before the problems caused by the forced use of the

Left: F.W. De Klerk takes the oath of office as president of South Africa. Right: Niili Taapopi is a member of Namibia's mission to the United Nations.

Afrikaans language in the school system, as well as the kind of education provided by South Africa, have been overcome.

The structure of medical facilities created by South Africa — first class for whites and inferior for blacks — will need a great deal of money and a whole new generation of medical workers before all Namibians can hope for good quality medical care.

During this period, South Africa will be undergoing its own transformation as it comes to grips with the prospect of majority rule. On March 17, 1992, South Africa's president, F. W. De Klerk, held a referendum in which the whites were asked if they wanted the government to go ahead with the reform process that was doing away with apartheid and to continue negotiations toward a new constitution that would give all citizens the vote. The answer was a resounding yes! Nearly 70 percent of the whites, including the Afrikaners, voted in favor of the reforms. These will lead to the first election that permits every adult citizen to vote, no later than 1994. The result is bound to have a big impact on Namibia. With a strong economy and a friendly multiracial government in South Africa, Namibia is sure to profit. After the vote was announced, Namibia's representative in the United States, Niili Taapopi, said, "If the whites had voted against the referendum, it would have been a catastrophe for us."

NAMIBIA AND THE WORLD

Namibia has had an unusual relationship with the rest of the world through the many years of its struggle for independence. It was the only country that the United Nations took as its direct responsibility. Though it was a colony of Germany for thirty years, it suffered another seventy-five years as a colony of another African country—South Africa. Because so many Namibians lived in exile, some for as long as thirty years, they learned a great deal about how to work with government officials, aid workers, and the United Nations representatives who assisted them in their push for independence. Namibia enjoys excellent relations with the United States, which worked for Namibian independence on many fronts. Namibia has always had a special relationship with the Scandinavian countries, which have contributed both money and education for the Namibians who were struggling through the years leading to independence. Finnish missionaries set up schools in Namibia that offered alternative education to those who wanted no part of the inferior system set up for blacks by South Africa. It is estimated that 90 percent of the people belong to one of the many churches there.

When Queen Elizabeth II of Great Britain visited Namibia in 1991, President Sam Nujoma escorted her on a tour.

COMMONWEALTH MEMBER

Immediately after gaining independence, Namibia applied to become a member of the British Commonwealth of Nations. This was a part of the government's plan to create bonds with the part of the world it admired. Niili Taapopi says, "We have a common history. We decided to take English as our official language. A lot of our people have received scholarships from Commonwealth nations." It was a way of starting over.

In honor of the Commonwealth's newest member, Britain's Queen Elizabeth II paid a formal state visit to the new nation. This joyous occasion helped Namibia in its efforts to find its way in the world. By joining the Commonwealth, Namibia became a member of a worldwide "club" whose membership now totals fifty countries.

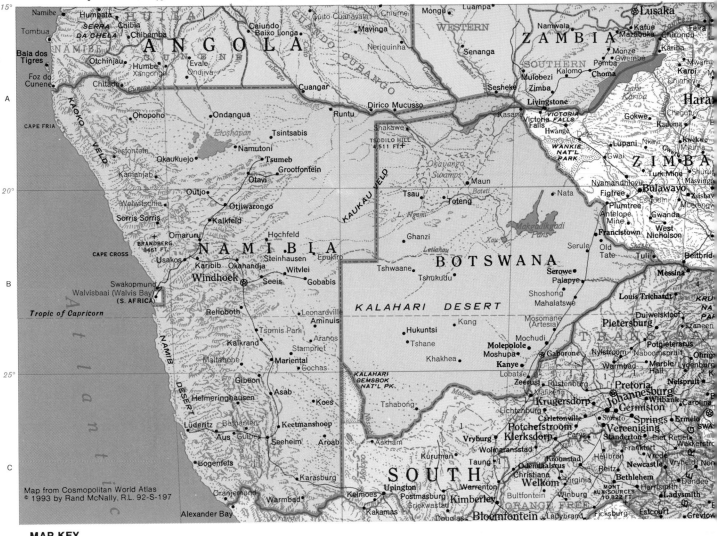

MAP KEY

MINI-FACTS AT A GLANCE

GENERAL INFORMATION

Official Name: Republic of Namibia

Capital: Windhoek

Government: Namibia is a unitary multiparty democratic republic with one legislative house—the National Assembly. The legislature consists of 72 elected and up to six appointed members. The National Council (a second legislative house), composed of two members from each of the country's 13 regions, are elected for a period of six years. The president is the head of state and head of the government, and the commander-in-chief of the defense forces. He is to be elected by the people for a term of five years and may serve a maximum of two five-year terms. For administrative purposes, the country is divided into 13 regions.

A Council of Traditional Chiefs is to be instituted to advise on issues of communal land.

Religion: There is no official religion, although some 90 percent of the population is Christian. The majority of the Christians are Lutheran, followed by Roman Catholic, Dutch Reformed, and Anglican. The rest of the population practice traditional African religions.

Language: At independence English was declared the official language. Most of the ethnic groups have their own languages; some 15 such languages are in use. Ovambo with its many dialects is the language of the majority of Namibians. Most of the whites and the Basters speak Afrikaans (a variation of Dutch) and German.

Money: South African rand (R) of 100 cents. In late 1991 one rand equaled $0.35 in United States currency. An independent currency is scheduled to be in circulation by the mid-1990s.

Weights and Measures: The metric system is in use.

Population: 1.78 million (1991); 32 percent urban and 68 percent rural; average population density 4.2 persons per sq. mi. (1.6 persons per sq km).

Cities:

Windhoek	114,500
Swakopmund	15,500
Rehoboth	15,000
Rundu	15,000
Keetmanshoop	14,000
Tsumeb	13,500
Otjiwarongo	11,000
Grootfontein	9,000

(Population figures based on 1990 estimates.)

GEOGRAPHY

Coastline: 950 mi. (1,500 km) along the Atlantic Ocean

Highest Point: Mt. Brandberg at 8,465 ft. (2,580 m)

Lowest Point: Sea level along the coast

Area: 317,818 sq. mi. (823,145 sq km)

Rivers: The Okavango and Kunene rivers form Namibia's northern border, the Zambezi the northeastern, and the Orange River forms its southern border. There are numerous seasonal waterbeds where rivers flow very briefly (2 to 3 days) after an occasional heavy rain. Lake Otjikoto and Lake Guinas are in the north. The Grootfontein area has considerable supplies of underground waters that can be obtained by sinking shallow wells.

Forests: Some 20 percent of the area is under forests and scrubland. The inland region gets barely enough rain to support small shrubs, trees, and grasslands. Desert vegetation consists of *Welwitschia mirabilis* and many varieties of aloe. The northern region supports deciduous, broad-leaved trees and a good growth of grasses. The bottle tree once provided poison used on the tips of arrows of San people; kokerboom trees provided wood for the arrows.

Wildlife: A great variety of wildlife exists in Namibia. Elephants, rhinoceroses, lions, cheetahs, leopards, ostriches, giraffes, zebras, kudu, elands, impalas, springboks, and wildebeests abound in game parks and grazing areas. Etosha National Park is one of Africa's best-run animal preserves. During the rainy season, flamingos gather by the thousands at Etosha. The Namib Desert Park is east of Swakopmund. Along with some tiny creatures like darkling beetles, jackals, hyenas, ostriches, and a few elephants and giraffes live in the Namib Desert region. A number of game reserves have been established in Namibia where hunting is strictly controlled and permitted only in designated areas.

Some 80,000 to 100,000 seals gather to feed and breed at the Cape Cross Seal Reserve on the Atlantic coast. The Bird Sanctuary at Walvis Bay attracts a large number of pelicans, flamingos, geese, cranes, cormorants, and some smaller seabirds.

Climate: Namibia has one of the driest climates in Africa. The climate in general is hot and dry with very little rainfall. Extremes of temperature are common. Temperatures can reach as high as 104° F (40° C) during the day, but nights can be very cold. The cold Benguela Current keeps the coast cool and damp. The rainy season lasts from December to March, but the rainfall is highly unreliable; rainfall ranges from 20 in. (50 cm) in the far north to about 1 in. to 5 in. (2.5 cm to 12 cm) in the south. Droughts are common. Some parts of Namibia do not get rain for decades.

Greatest Distance: East to West: about 880 mi. (1,420 km)
North to South: 820 mi. (1,320 km)

ECONOMY AND INDUSTRY

Agriculture: Less than 1 percent of the land is under agriculture and permanent cultivation. Subsistence agriculture (raising of just enough crops for farmers and their families) is confined to the north. The generally dry and unfertile land yields some maize (corn), millet, sorghum, other vegetables, melons and other fruits, and *pulses*, edible seeds of pod-bearing plants. A tomato farm and a canning factory operate in the south along the border with South Africa.

Large modern white-owned ranches raise livestock, chiefly for export. Karakul sheep raising is centered in the more arid southern region. The Herero own large herds of cattle and they have cattle auctions two or three times a year. About 65 percent of the land is used for pasture and grazing land. Livestock includes cattle, sheep, goats, horses, mules, and pigs. Livestock products of karakul pelts and meat account for more than half of the value of agricultural production.

The fishing industry is based at Luderitz and Walvis Bay. Namibia claims two hundred nautical miles of Exclusive Economic Zone (EEZ) along the Atlantic Coast. Fish catch consists of Cape horse mackerel, anchovies, pilchards (sardines), maasbanker tuna, Cape hake, and crab

Mining: Namibia has rich mineral deposits. Mining is the most important economic activity, contributing some 75 percent of the total exports. Uranium deposits at Rossing are the largest-known in the world. Diamonds (mostly of gem quality), zinc, lead, copper, uranium, gold, and silver are the chief minerals. Namibia has the world's richest alluvial deposits of gem diamonds. Tin, vanadium, semiprecious gemstones, lithium, pyrite, tantalite, phosphate, sulfur, and salt are also important. Large areas, including offshore, are being explored for oil and gas.

Manufacturing: The manufacturing sector is rather small. Gem cutting (mostly diamonds), karakul fur products, and meat processing are the primary light manufacturing activities. Processing of fish meat and dairy products, textiles, carved wood products, metal refining, beer brewing, and clothing are also important.

Transportation: Namibia is well connected by roads and railways with South Africa. There are some 25,983 mi. (41,815 km) of roads, about 10 percent of which are paved. More than 2,000 mi. (3,218 km) of railroads connect major economic and population centers with the South African rail system. Air Namibia flies to major cities in the neighboring African countries and to Frankfurt, Germany. Windhoek is the largest airport, served by several international airlines. There are 11 other airports with scheduled flights. Walvis Bay, officially part of South Africa, is the chief port.

Communication: There are about five daily newspapers. The Namibia Broadcasting Corporation runs the television and radio network. The radio broadcasts in 12 languages. In the early 1990s there were six people per radio receiver, 42 persons per television set, and some 18 persons per telephone.

Trade: Food and other consumer goods form the largest group of import items. Other imports include fuel and transportation equipment. South Africa is the largest import source. Exports include minerals (diamonds and uranium), fish, beef cattle, and karakul pelts. Chief export destinations are the United States, Germany, South Africa, and Japan.

EVERYDAY LIFE

Health: By many economic and social indicators, Namibia is better off than many black African countries, but within the country there is a great disparity between whites and blacks and rural and urban Namibia. The majority of the health facilities are in towns and bigger cities. Efforts are being made to establish clinics all over the populated areas that can offer basic care. The major diseases are malaria (mostly in the north), tuberculosis, and trypanosomiasis (sleeping sickness).

Education: Education was administered by several ethnically-based authorities prior to independence. It is now officially compulsory and free for 9 years between the ages of 7 and 16. Primary education, beginning at 7 years of age, lasts for 7 years; secondary education begins at the age of 14 and lasts for 5 years. Most of the mining companies offer education facilities in the mining towns. Higher education is provided by the University of Namibia, several teacher-training colleges, technical institutes, and agricultural colleges.

Holidays:

New Year's Day, January 1
Independence Day, March 21
Easter Sunday, usually in March or April
Worker's Day, May 1
Ascension Day, May 9
Namibia Day, August 26
Human Rights Day, December 10
Christmas, December 25-26

Culture: Most of the cities and towns have libraries. The National Museum and Archives are in Windhoek and two local museums are in Luderitz and Swakopmund. The National Theater of Namibia presents plays depicting both village life and contemporary living. In rural areas traditional ways are still an important part of everyday life. Handicrafts like basket weaving and pottery are part of daily life in Namibia. Folk art objects are displayed at the National Crafts Center in Windhoek.

Food: Although Namibia produces some food grains, most of the food needed is imported. Millet is an important part of the Namibian diet. Corn flour, groundnuts (peanuts), sorghum, beans, cassava, and milk are also used in daily food. *Biltong*, a kind of beef jerky, is a popular food item.

Sports and Recreation: Namibia actively sought inclusion in the 1992 Summer Olympics held in Barcelona, Spain. A team of runners, swimmers, and boxers represented their country. Soccer, known as football, is considered the national sport. In 1992 the Paris-Cape Town auto rally was extended to the south of the continent, including Namibia.

IMPORTANT DATES

1484—Portuguese land on the Atlantic coast just north of the present-day town of Swakopmund; Diogo Cão, a Portuguese mariner, becomes the first white man to arrive in South West Africa

1486 — Portuguese sailor Bartholomew Diaz lands near the present-day town of Luderitz

1834 — The Wesleyans (Methodists) open a mission among the Nama people

1840 — The Nama defeat the Herero and push them north of the Swakop River

1842 — The Wesleyan Mission is taken over by the Rhenish Missionary Society

1858 — Nama chiefs are united in their desire not to sell any of their land to whites

1860 — Keetmanshoop town is founded

1863 — Fighting starts once again between Herero and Nama

1868 — Germans start colonizing Namibia's coast

1870 — Baster leader obtains the town of Rehoboth

1878 — United Kingdom annexes Walvis Bay on behalf of Cape Colony

1883 — Adolf Luderitz buys land around Angra Pequena to develop as a port; he establishes a trading post

1884 — Germany calls "Berlin West African Conference"; South West Africa becomes a German possession

1889 — German soldiers are called in to control South West Africa

1890 — Chief Maharero, who was also called Kamaharero, dies and is succeeded by his son Samuel Maharero; Caprivi Strip is given by the British to the German colonial government in exchange for the island of Zanzibar; German Chancellor von Caprivi declares that he will control South West Africa "at all costs"

1895 — Rhenish Mission Church building is built

1898 — Theodor Leutwein is appointed governor of the territory

1899 — War breaks out between Boers and English-speaking people in South Africa (ends 1902)

1902 — Treaty of Vereeniging

1904 — Herero revolt against German occupation; Battle of Hamakari

1905 — Some 80 percent of Herero are killed in the revolt against Germans

1907 — Germans crush Herero revolt

1908 — Diamonds are discovered for the first time at Luderitz

1914 — South African forces occupy South West Africa

1915 — Germany surrenders the territory of South West Africa

1920 — Under Article 22 of the Covenant of the League of Nations, administration of South West Africa is given to South Africa; it requires that South Africa promotes the utmost material and moral well being and social progress of the people; Consolidated Diamond Mines (CDM) is created

1928 — South Africa grants limited self-government rights to European inhabitants only; Consolidated Diamond Mines (CDM) starts operation

1931 — British Parliament recognizes South Africa's independence

1945 — United Nations (UN) replaces the League of Nations

1946 — UN refuses South Africa's request to annex South West Africa

1948 — Balance of power shifts from English-speaking whites to more conservative Afrikaners in South Africa; South Africa's security and apartheid laws, mandating separation of the races, are extended to South West Africa

1949 — The territory's European voters are granted representation in the South African Parliament

1950 — The International Court of Justice (ICJ) issues a ruling that South Africa should submit South West Africa to the UN

1957 — Ovamboland People's Organization (OPO), a labor movement, is launched

1959 — South West African National Union (SWANU) is formed; 13 people are killed and more than a hundred are wounded while protesting takeover of their township by the white Windhoek administration

1960 — OPO is renamed South West African People's Organization (SWAPO) and it expands its platform to combat racial segregation, land appropriation, and restrictions on freedom of movement

1961 — South Africa drops out of the British Commonwealth; Wolfgang Delfs begins a private game reserve

1966 — SWAPO announces armed struggle for the liberation of South West Africa

1967 — UN Council for Namibia is established

1968 — South West Africa is formally renamed Namibia by UN General Assembly resolution

1971 — The ICJ rules South Africa's presence in Namibia is illegal and therefore it should withdraw from Namibia immediately; workers stage a massive and long strike (ended in 1972) against South African occupation

1973—UN General Assembly recognizes SWAPO as the authentic representative of the Namibian people; UN appoints the first UN commissioner for Namibia; South Africa establishes a short-lived multiracial Advisory Council for the territory

1974—Natural gas is discovered in a well off the mouth of the Orange River

1975—Turnhalle Conference starts in Windhoek; Angola becomes independent

1977—South Africa appoints an administrator general to govern the territory of South West Africa; Turnhalle Conference is dissolved; South Africa creates a "security zone" along the Angola border; South Africa reannexes the enclave of Walvis Bay; Canada, France, West Germany, United Kingdom, and the United States launch a joint diplomatic effort to bring independence

1978—Proposal 435 is approved in the UN Security Council for settling Namibia's problems; South African-backed elections are held in Namibia, UN regards these elections null and void; some 20,000 South African troops are stationed in Namibia; large parts of the north are put under martial law; uranium mine at Rossing starts production

1979—South Africa unilaterally establishes a legislative National Assembly, without executive powers, for Namibia

1980—National Assembly in Namibia creates a military draft for all men between the ages of 16 and 25

1981—A conference is arranged by the UN in Geneva, Switzerland, for all parties; South Africa attacks military installations in Angola; television relays start from South Africa

1982—United States puts forward a proposal linking Namibian independence with the withdrawal of Cuban troops from Angola; a constitution is drafted; the Namibian Wildlife Trust is organized

1984—Angola agrees to the withdrawal of Cuban troops

1988—South Africa agrees to a plan to free Namibia by April 1990; CDM opens a diamond sorting house in Windhoek

1989—SWAPO and South Africa agree to a cease-fire; elections are held for a Constituent assembly; SWAPO wins more than half the vote

1990—In accord with the plan outlined in the United Nations Security Council Resolution number 435, Namibia becomes an independent nation; a new constitution is drafted and adopted; Namibia joins the International Monetary Fund (IMF); it also becomes the 50th member of the British Commonwealth and the 160th member of the United Nations; the national flag is adopted; Sam Nujoma, the leader of SWAPO, is chosen the country's first president

1991 — Future ownership of the Walvis Bay is discussed at the talks between Namibia and South Africa; CDM opens a diamond mine at Elizabeth Bay, near Luderitz

1992 — Namibia suffers one of the worst droughts in the 20th century; 80 percent of country's corn crop is lost to drought; a 13-million-year-old jawbone of a hominid is found in the Otavi region during an anthropological expedition; Michelle McLean, a white Namibian teenager, is crowned Miss Universe; Frankie Fredericks wins 2 silver medals in track and field in the 25th modern Olympics

1993 — South Africa agrees to turn over control of Walvis Bay to Namibia, with the transfer probably to occur in 1994

IMPORTANT PEOPLE

Martti Ahtisaari, special United Nations representative appointed to oversee UN presence in Namibia in 1978

Sir Henry Barkly, British governor of the Cape Colony

Otto von Bismarck (1815-1898), German Chancellor

Leo von Caprivi, German Chancellor

Roelof "Pik" Botha, South Africa's foreign minister during the end of the twentieth century

Johannes Marthinus De Wet (1927-   ), commissioner-general of South West Africa in the 1970s

Wolfgang Delfs, a Namibian farmer of German origin; supplies wild animals to safari parks and zoos

Frankie Fredericks, popular sports figure, sometimes called Africa's fastest man, won 2 silver medals in track and field in the 1992 Olympics

Hage Gottfried Geingob, first prime minister of independent Namibia

Dr. Richard Hindorf, a German consultant who advised German businessmen how to get the most out of their investments in South West Africa in the 1890s

Clemens Kapuuo (1923-78), a paramount chief of the Herero in the 1970s

Peter Hitjitevi Katjavivi (1941-   ), leader of SWAPO and vice-chancellor of the University of Namibia

F. W. De Klerk, South Africa's president in the early 1990s

Hosea Kutako (1869?-1971), a paramount chief of the Herero from 1923 to 1971, considered the father of nationalism in Namibia

Theodor Leutwein, German governor of the territory of South West Africa in the 1890s

Adolf Luderitz, a German merchant; developed a harbor near Angra Pequena; town of Luderitz is named after him

Maharero (1820?-90), also called Kamaharero, a paramount chief of the Herero from 1861 to 1890

Samuel Maharero (?-1923), a Herero chief in the 1890s; died in exile in Botswana

Dirk Mudge, a white political leader of the Democratic Turnhalle Alliance (DTA) party

Misheke Muyongo (1940-   ), leader of the Democratic Turnhalle Alliance (DTA) party

Sam Shafilshuna Nujoma (1929-   ), Namibia's president; also president of SWAPO

Louise Pienaar, South African administrator-general of South West Africa until March 21, 1990

Hifikepunye Lucas Pohamba (1935-   ), SWAPO member, minister of Home Affairs

Marthinus Steyn, South African justice, appointed as administrator-general of South West Africa

Niili Taapopi, Namibia's representative to the United Nations in the early 1990s

Andimba Herman Toivo ja Toivo (1924-   ), Minister of Mines and Energy; the founder of SWAPO (South West Africa People's Organization), and the leader of Namibian nationalism; in prison as political prisoner from 1966 to 1984

von Trotha, German general in the early 1900s; he ordered extermination of Herero nation in October 1904

John Vorster, South African president in the 1970s

Barend Johannes Van der Walt (1928-   ), South Africa's administrator of South West Africa in the 1970s

Hendrik Witbooi (1825-1905), a Nama chief with great military skills

Elias Aro Xoagub, Namibian farmer; *Twyfelfontein* rock paintings are located on his farm

Andrew Young (1932-   ), US clergyman, civil rights leader, congressman, and mayor; US ambassador to the UN in the 1970s

INDEX

Page numbers that appear in boldface type indicate illustrations

About the Author

Jason Lauré was born in Chehalis, Washington, and lived in California before joining the United States army and serving in France. He attended Columbia University and worked for *The New York Times*. He traveled to San Francisco and became a photographer during the turbulent 1960s. He recorded those events before setting out on the first of many trips to Africa.

Mr. Lauré covers the political life of that continent and also has made a number of expeditions across the Sahara. He has written about, and photographed in, forty countries in Africa. He has written three books, published by Farrar, Straus & Giroux Inc., on South Africa, Portugal, and Bangladesh, in collaboration with Ettagale Blauer. Their Bangladesh book was nominated for a National Book Award.

In the Enchantment of the World series, Mr. Lauré has written the books on Zimbabwe, Bangladesh, Angola, and Zambia.

Mr. Lauré is married to Marisia Lauré, a translator.